Ramses II

AND EGYPT

Olivier Tiano

Art direction by Michel Coudeyre

A Henry Holt Reference Book

Henry Holt and Company

New York

A
PICTURE
IS WORTH
A THOUSAND
WORDS

Xun Zi (313-238 B.C.)

聞者不若見之

中耀書箇子語录

Henry Holt and Company, Inc.
Publishers since 1866
115 West 18th Street
New York, New York 10011

Henry Holt® is a registered trademark
of Henry Holt and Company, Inc.

Copyright © 1995 by Editions Mango
American English translation copyright © 1996 by
Henry Holt and Company, Inc.
All rights reserved.
Published in Canada by Fitzhenry & Whiteside Ltd.,
195 Allstate Parkway, Markham, Ontario L3R 4T8.

Library of Congress Cataloging-in-Publication Data
Tiano, Olivier.
[Ramsès II et son temps. English]
Ramses II and Egypt / Olivier Tiano.—1st American ed.
p. cm.
—(W5 (who, what, where, when, and why) series)
Includes bibliographical references (p.) and index.
1. Ramses II, King of Egypt. 2. Egypt—Civilization—
To 332 B.C.
I. Title. II. Series
DT88.T513   1996   95-40017
932'.014'092—dc20   CIP
ISBN 0-8050-4659-3

Henry Holt books are available for special
promotions and premiums.
For details contact: Director, Special Markets.

Originally published in France in 1996 by
Editions Mango under the title *Ramsès II et Son Temps*.

First published in the United States in 1996 by
Henry Holt and Company, Inc.

First American Edition—1996

Art direction by Michel Coudeyre
Idea and series by Dominique Gaussen
American English translation by Constantin Marinescu

Historical consultant, J.H. Sibal

Typesetting by Jay Hyams and Christopher Hyams Hart

Printed in France
All first editions are printed on acid-free paper.∞
1 2 3 4 5 6 7 8 9 10

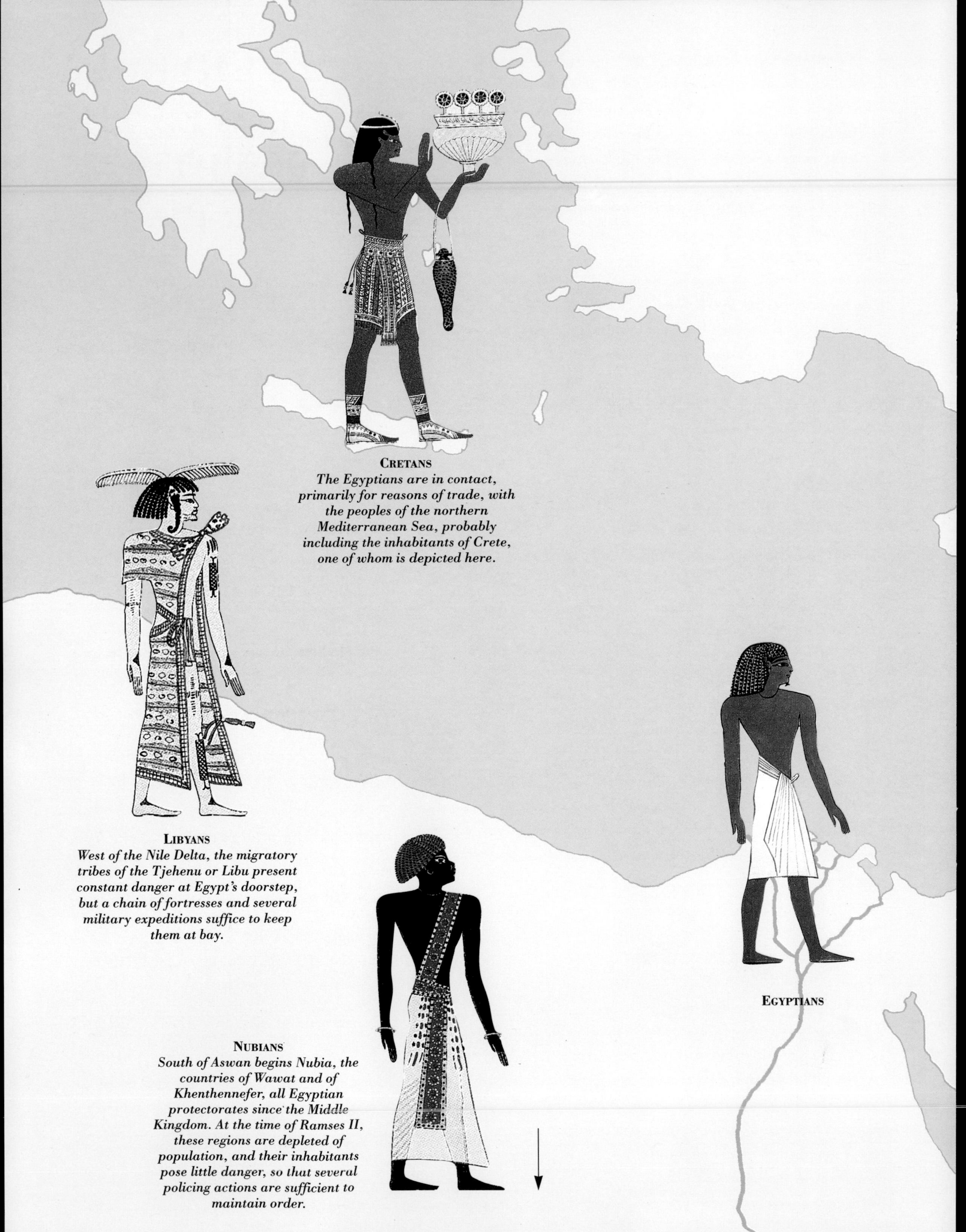

CRETANS

The Egyptians are in contact, primarily for reasons of trade, with the peoples of the northern Mediterranean Sea, probably including the inhabitants of Crete, one of whom is depicted here.

LIBYANS

West of the Nile Delta, the migratory tribes of the Tjehenu or Libu present constant danger at Egypt's doorstep, but a chain of fortresses and several military expeditions suffice to keep them at bay.

EGYPTIANS

NUBIANS

South of Aswan begins Nubia, the countries of Wawat and of Khenthennefer, all Egyptian protectorates since the Middle Kingdom. At the time of Ramses II, these regions are depleted of population, and their inhabitants pose little danger, so that several policing actions are sufficient to maintain order.

HITTITES
North of the land of the Naharina the Hittite Empire begins. The Hittites are Egypt's most dangerous adversary on the eve of Ramses II's ascension to the throne. The inevitable confrontation will take place at Kadesh.

ASIATICS
The region of the western coast of Asia, the land located between the Sinai desert and the mountains of Lebanon, is an Egyptian protectorate, but the populations of Retenu and Naharina must frequently be subdued by shows of force.

EVERYBODY LOVES THE EGYPTIANS, RIGHT?

When Ramses II ascends the throne, Egypt is a prosperous country, the leading power in the Near East. Located in Africa, the Egyptian Empire extends south to the Fourth Cataract of the Nile. Connected to Asia by the Isthmus of Suez, Egypt controls the Mediterranean coast up to the Orontes River. Enriched by the fertility of its soil and by the riches won by its warrior pharaohs, Egypt draws to it products from the Mediterranean Sea, Asia, and the interior of Africa. But its power is fragile, threatened by neighbors who watch closely for any sign of weakness, a weakness that will come less than a century after the death of Ramses II.

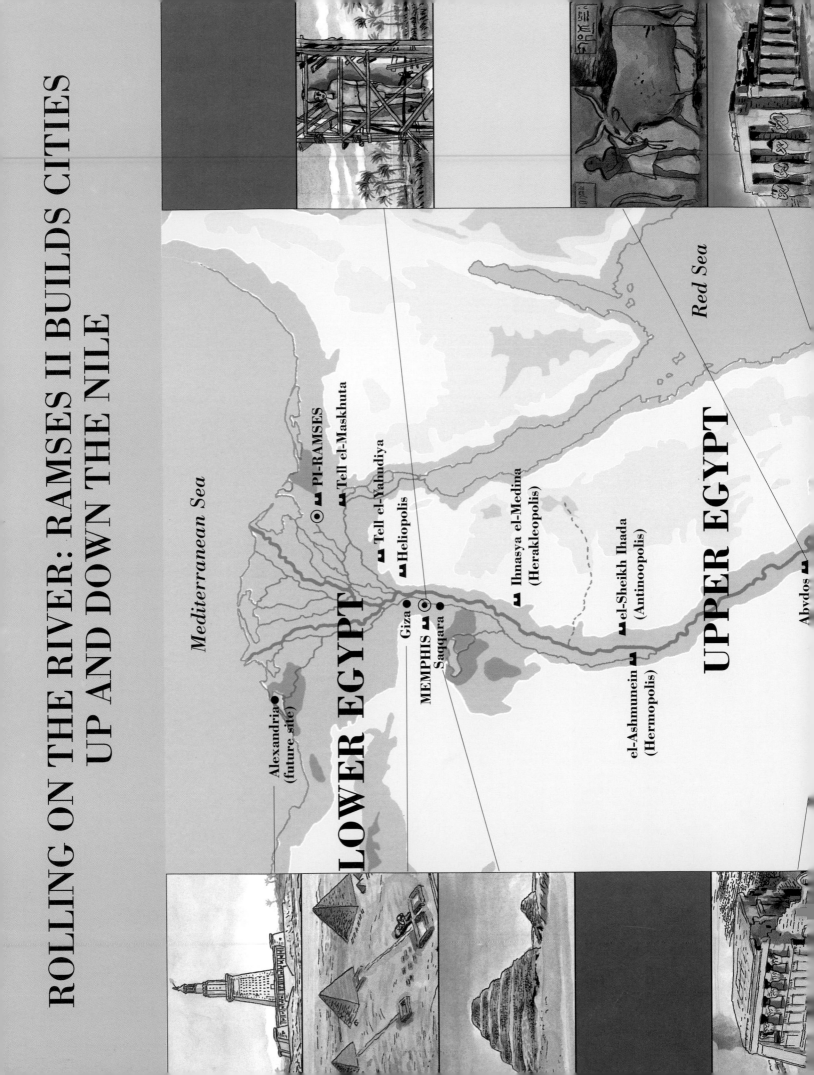

ROLLING ON THE RIVER: RAMSES II BUILDS CITIES UP AND DOWN THE NILE

Mediterranean Sea

Red Sea

LOWER EGYPT

UPPER EGYPT

Alexandria● (future site)

◉ PI-RAMSES

Tell el-Maskhuta

Tell el-Yahudiya

Heliopolis

Giza●
MEMPHIS ◉
Saqqara●

Ihnasya el-Medina (Herakleopolis)

el-Sheikh Ibada (Antinoopolis)

el-Ashmunein (Hermopolis)

Abydos

Buildings from the period of Ramses II

Buildings from before or after Ramses II

Tukh

Ramesseum

⊙THEBES
Karnak
Luxor
El-Kab

Edfu

Philae

Beit el-Wali

Gerf Hussein

Quban

Wadi el-Sobua

el-Derr

Abu Simbel
Faras
Aksha

NUBIA

Amara West
Per-Ramses-Meryamon

Gebel Barkal
(Napata)

⊙ Capitals of Ramses II
◢ Built by Ramses II
● Other ancient sites

THE NILE: A MIRACLE 1,200 MILES LONG AND 12 MILES WIDE

Egypt is a "gift of the Nile." This statement, attributed to the Greek historian Herodotus, accurately captures

the spirit of the kingdom. From north to south, Egypt comprises mainly the valley of the Nile. The river is the

source of all life, and the land owes its bountiful richness to the summer flooding of the waters. The god that

the ancient Egyptians believe represents this phenomenon is Hapy, a male divinity with hanging breasts that

symbolize the nourishing character of the river. The Nile valley has a width of only about six miles from Aswan

to Cairo, the area known as Upper Egypt, and develops into a marshy delta between Cairo and the

Mediterranean Sea, the area called Lower Egypt. Vast deserts extend beyond the waters on both sides of the

river, their aridity broken only by an occasional oasis connected to the Nile valley by paths lined by watering

holes; these watering holes are nearly always controlled by hostile Bedouins (desert-dwelling nomads), over

whom the pharaohs must keep a watchful eye. From the Atlantic to the Caucasus, the huge deserts are inter-

rupted only occasionally by the miracle of water. In Africa this miracle is named the Nile. The river is the dispenser of life, a divine river that is a strong reason behind the political unification and wealth of Egypt. The flooding of the waters allows the soil to be irrigated and enriched, but to better take advantage of this a central authority is needed to maintain dams and channels along the river's course. The Nile stands as the backbone of the entire country, providing the main means of communication.

You could travel on its banks by foot or donkey, but any important load, any majestic procession, must use the water.

To transport the stones of the pyramids, the obelisks of the temples, or the blocks destined for huge royal statues, barges are used on the river when its flooding brings the waters to the borders of the lands where divine temples and funeral monuments of the kings are to be erected. For the job of ferrying divine statues from one temple to the other only ceremonial barges are used, vessels encrusted with gold and silver and decorated with multicolored fabrics.

In 1954, at the foot of the pyramid of Cheops in Giza, two large pits containing a pair of large royal ships are discovered. One of these has been exhumed and has a length of more than 130 feet. It is made from more than 1,200 pieces of wood, mainly cedar imported from Lebanon, the pieces bound to one another by ropes. The prevalence of navigation in daily life, from the peasant on his small papyrus boat to the pharaoh riding on his ship of rare wood, has a direct correspondence to the worship of their gods. Thus the sun god Ra who travels across the sky in the shape of a falcon flying in the air is frequently represented in a sky, or celestial,

boat sailing along the starry body of his mother, the sky goddess Nut. Most ancient Egyptian myths about the creation of the world imagine life and order coming out of the chaos and nothingness of a primordial ocean, an ocean that for the Egyptians must surely have been the Nile.

IN THE SKY AND ON THE EARTH, ON THE

THE SCARAB
Because this beetle rolls a ball of dung in front of it, it is associated with Khepri, the rising sun.

THE WILD CAT
The wild cat has not been domesticated, but its gentler distant cousin is much appreciated by the Egyptians, who call it "meow."

THE FALCON
Always present in the Egyptian sky, which it seems to rule, the falcon is the symbol of many divinities, including Horus, the protector of the Egyptian monarchy.

RIVER'S BANK AND IN THE DESERT . . .

THE WILD VULTURE
Long the symbol of Nekhebet, the goddess of Upper Egypt, the vulture is also the animal form of the goddess Mut, wife of the god Amun of Thebes.

THE LION
A majestic animal, the lion is associated with the pharaoh, to whom the lion lends strength. The lion is also guardian of the sun.

THE HORNED VIPER WITH ITS DEADLY VENOM
This snake is used for writing the letter F, but even so it seems dangerous to scribes, who occasionally represent it cut in pieces in order to cleanse its image of any harmful powers.

11

. . . THE UNIVERSE OF THE

THE BABOON
Baboons are believed to be sun worshipers because they shout at sunrise and sunset. Because of their tranquility they are also associated with the god of the scribes, Thoth.

THE EGYPTIAN VULTURE
In contrast to the wild vulture, the Egyptian does not lend its shape to any deity. It is the image of the hieroglyph Aleph, the first sign of the Egyptian "alphabet."

THE COBRA
This is the symbol of the goddess of Lower Egypt, always depicted in the shape of a threatening serpent, its hood expanded, ready to spit venom at an enemy.

PAPYRUS
This is the plant symbol of Lower Egypt. It is one of the essential materials of everyday life, supplying the material used by scribes and also used to make small fishing boats.

EGYPTIANS IS FULL OF GODS

THE IBIS
The big white ibis is the bird of the moon god Thoth. Thousands of its mummies have been found. The bird's Egyptian name, Heby, is the source of our word ibis.

THE ASHY HERON
This is the sacred bird of the sun at Heliopolis. Perched on the banks of earth that emerge from the flood waters of the Nile, it is the symbol of the sun emerging from the primordial ocean at the creation of world. It is similar to the phoenix of the Greeks.

THE HIPPOPOTAMUS
Hunted with spears since the earliest days, the hippopotamus is identified with the negative forces in the universe. Even so, the female hippopotamus has become identified with a very popular goddess, Taweret, who watches over women and children.

COMPARED TO EGYPTIAN HISTORY,
THAN THE SIZE OF

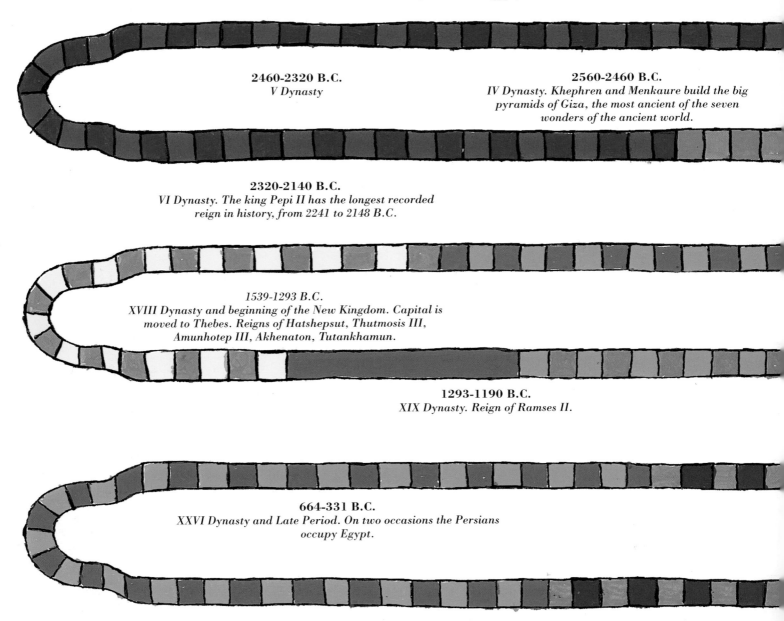

Circa 3200 B.C.
The appearance of hieroglyphic writing and the division of Egypt into two kingdoms: Upper Egypt, from Aswan to Cairo, and Lower Egypt, the Nile Delta.

2460-2320 B.C.
V Dynasty

2560-2460 B.C.
IV Dynasty. Khephren and Menkaure build the big pyramids of Giza, the most ancient of the seven wonders of the ancient world.

2320-2140 B.C.
VI Dynasty. The king Pepi II has the longest recorded reign in history, from 2241 to 2148 B.C.

1539-1293 B.C.
XVIII Dynasty and beginning of the New Kingdom. Capital is moved to Thebes. Reigns of Hatshepsut, Thutmosis III, Amunhotep III, Akhenaton, Tutankhamun.

1293-1190 B.C.
XIX Dynasty. Reign of Ramses II.

664-331 B.C.
XXVI Dynasty and Late Period. On two occasions the Persians occupy Egypt.

The Egyptians don't have a continuous chronology. Their years are dated starting from the beginning of each new pharaoh's reign. In the third century B.C. a Hellenized Egyptian priest named Manetho writes a history of Egypt in which he groups the pharaohs into 31 dynasties, the last one being that of the Ptolemies, the sovereigns of Macedonian origin who are the kings of Egypt after Alexander the Great's reign. The nature of the transition from one dynasty to the next remains mysterious. In most cases a dynasty corresponds to a family originating in a particular city.

Egyptologists have regrouped these dynasties into larger periods. Those that correspond to a strong central power are called "kingdoms": the Old, Middle, and New kingdoms. Those that are plagued by anarchy and foreign invasions

MOST CIVILIZATIONS ARE NO LONGER AN EARTHWORM

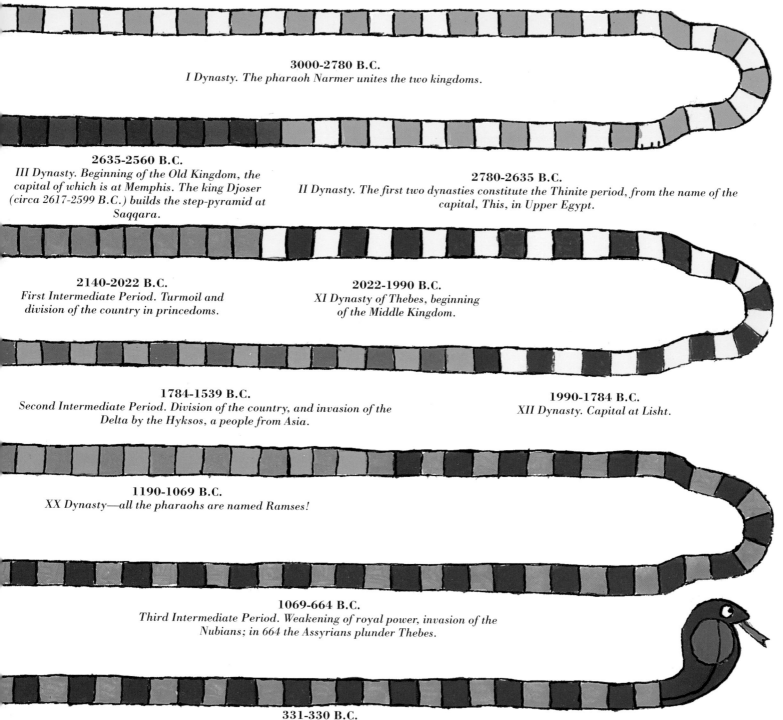

3000-2780 B.C.
I Dynasty. The pharaoh Narmer unites the two kingdoms.

2635-2560 B.C.
III Dynasty. Beginning of the Old Kingdom, the capital of which is at Memphis. The king Djoser (circa 2617-2599 B.C.) builds the step-pyramid at Saqqara.

2780-2635 B.C.
II Dynasty. The first two dynasties constitute the Thinite period, from the name of the capital, This, in Upper Egypt.

2140-2022 B.C.
First Intermediate Period. Turmoil and division of the country in princedoms.

2022-1990 B.C.
XI Dynasty of Thebes, beginning of the Middle Kingdom.

1784-1539 B.C.
Second Intermediate Period. Division of the country, and invasion of the Delta by the Hyksos, a people from Asia.

1990-1784 B.C.
XII Dynasty. Capital at Lisht.

1190-1069 B.C.
XX Dynasty—all the pharaohs are named Ramses!

1069-664 B.C.
Third Intermediate Period. Weakening of royal power, invasion of the Nubians; in 664 the Assyrians plunder Thebes.

331-330 B.C.
Alexander the Great defeats the Persians. The beginning of the Ptolemaic period. The Ptolemies transform Alexandria into the cultural capital of the Mediterranean world and construct its famous lighthouse, one of the seven wonders of the ancient world. In 30 B.C., Cleopatra commits suicide after being defeated by Octavian (Augustus). This is the end of Egyptian independence.

are called "intermediate periods." After the Third Intermediate Period, a time of confusion with alternating periods of national rule and foreign occupation leads to the creation of what is vaguely designated as the "Late Period." On the death of Alexander the Great, his empire is divided; Egypt is given to one of his generals, Ptolemy, the son of Lagus, whose rule begins the XXXI Dynasty, known also as the Ptolemaic Dynasty or Lagid Period. With the suicide of the last Ptolemaic sovereign, Cleopatra VII, Egypt falls into the hands of the Romans and loses its independence. The emperors of Rome will be represented as pharaohs on the walls of Egyptian temples, but after three thousand years of history "pharaonic" Egypt no longer exists.

King Seti I commissions artists to memorialize him in his temple at Abydos together with his son, the future Ramses II, in front of a list of all their ancestors. This is an impressive gallery of 75 cartouches (decorated panels) bearing the names of the most prestigious pharaohs going back to the founder of the Egyptian kingdom, the legendary Menes (or Narmer). In this monument Seti I creates an official genealogy that is not exactly accurate. In Egypt, a pharaoh cannot be of plebeian origin, and thus the hunt for noble ancestors begins. But what is the true origin of the family of Ramses II? In fact, its history is related to the decline of the XVIII Dynasty after the reign of the pharaoh Akhenaton

HISTORIES, AND THE TRUTH

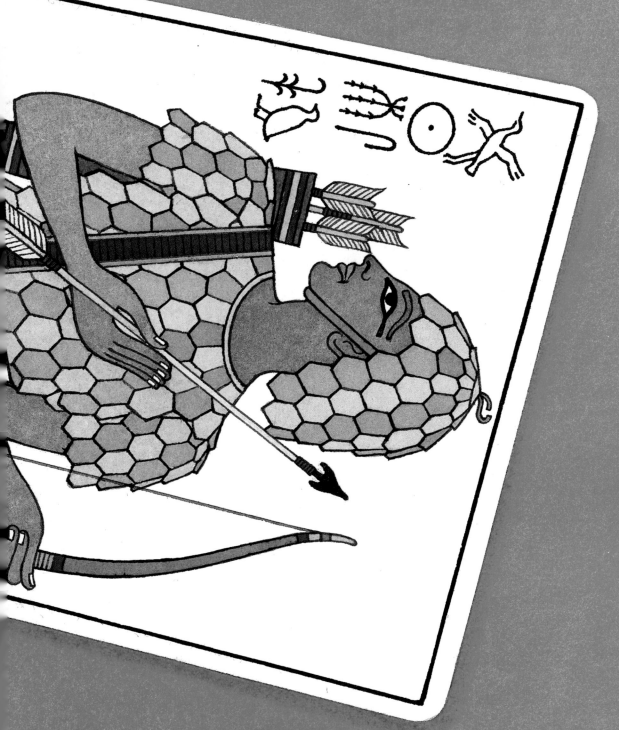

and his successor, Tutankhamun, who dies without leaving a male heir. A priest by the name of Ay ascends to the throne and marries a royal princess in order to legitimate his reign. After his death, the general Horemheb gains power using the same method. Before dying he leaves the throne to another soldier, Paramessu, who becomes Ramses I. This is the beginning of the XIX Dynasty. His son Seti I succeeds him, and after Seti's death the throne goes to his son, Ramses II. Their somewhat humdrum origins are now forgotten, and a new royal family is born that traces its name back to glorious ancestors, pyramid builders and conquerors of the entire known world.

HORUS
"Powerful bull, beloved of Maat"

THE ONE OF TWO GODDESSES*
"Protector of Egypt, who subdues foreign countries"
* The vulture-goddess of Upper Egypt and the cobra-goddess of Lower Egypt.

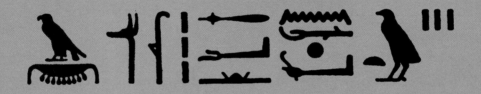

GOLDEN HORUS
"Rich in years, great in victories"

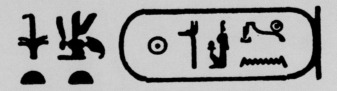

THE ONE OF THE REED AND THE BEE*
"Powerful is the Maat (truth-justice) of Ra, the Elect of Ra"
* The reed of Upper Egypt and the bee of Lower Egypt; usually translated as the king of Upper and Lower Egypt.

SON OF RA
"Ra has given birth to him*, loved by Amun"
* Translation of Ramses' name

18

A PHARAOH CAN'T HAVE JUST ONE NAME

When Prince Ramses comes to the throne after the death of his father, Seti I, he has to follow tradition and adopt a royal title by adding another four names to the one he has had since birth. According to ancient custom, his majesty, the pharaoh, is vested with an entire program of five names. The names themselves—"Horus," "The One of Two Goddesses," "Golden Horus," "The One of the Reed and the Bee," and "Son of Ra"—relate the new pharaoh to the protector divinities of Egypt's royalty. Their signification has the same effect: Ramses is born from the god Ra, the sun-god of Heliopolis, he is loved by the god Amun, the master of the capital Thebes, as well as by Maat, the goddess who symbolizes the Truth and Justice required to maintain cosmic order.

However, the king is also placed in a more earthly context through the affirmation of his strength. He is the "powerful bull," the one who "subdues foreign countries" and the protector of Egypt by his victories.

What about the title *pharaoh*? Ramses is styled as Horus, king of Upper and Lower Egypt, protected by the Two Goddesses, and son of Ra, but nowhere is he called "pharaoh." In fact, this term, which we customarily use today to designate the kings of ancient Egypt, does not appear before 1000 B.C. In some Late Period temples it is encircled by a cartouche and replaced the name of the king of that time. The word *pharaoh* means literally "great house," the royal palace, and its use is similar to the term White House in the United States or Elysium (the Parisian residence of the president) in France, both of which designate the nation's executive power.

According to the documents of his reign, Ramses II ascends the throne of Egypt at the beginning of June 1279 and dies early in August 1213, which means he rules for 66 years and two months. This matches the statements of the priest Manetho in the history of Egypt he writes during the third century B.C. This exceptionally long reign is exceeded by only one other pharaoh, Pepi II of the VI Dynasty, who is recorded as having been in power for 94 years.

The numerous monuments on which the king leaves his imprint, as well as all those that he has built, are testaments to his activity as a builder.. But what is he known for during his life?

Throughout his lifetime, the fame of Ramses II rests primarily on the events at Kadesh and his reputation as a warrior. Even so, after his tenth year of reign the king doesn't undertake any military action of great importance except for a policing expedition in Nubia in year 19 or 20 (remember, the Egyptians number years from the beginning of the pharaoh's reign). In fact, the Hittite king Muwatallis, his most determined adversary, dies in year 10. This state of "no war" was ratified in year 21 by a peace treaty with the kingdom of Hatti, consolidated by a marriage with a Hittite princess in 34, confirmed by a visit from the Hittite prince-heir to Egypt in 38, as well as strengthened through a second marriage around 40-42. Ultimately, this warrior seems to have been more of a diplomat, as befits his role of head of state. During these numerous years of peace, the king's main concern seems to be the assertion of his divine nature, by means of his monuments and his statues, as well as on the occasion of *sed* feasts, the ceremonies designated to affirm and renew the powers of the king. Ramses celebrates more of these jubilees than any other king. The first one takes place, according to tradition, in the thirtieth year of his reign, but twelve others are organized later and proclaimed throughout the entire country. Because the *sed* feasts deal with the divine origin of the pharaoh's power, they provide a unique opportunity to make a god out of Ramses. However, the king does not wait for his first *sed*. The temple of Abu Simbel is officially inaugurated in year 24, and here the king is already represented as a god. As a living god he is the

OF RAMSES II

object of a cult, and huge statues with his effigy bear evocative names: "Ramses Meryamon, the god," "King of Kings," "Montu, in the double country," and so on. You might ask how long Ramses actually directs the course of the state. The absence of important events after the treaty with the Hittites, the activities of some other princes, and the power of a small number of high dignitaries suggest that the king—burdened by the prestige of his exploits—progressively delegates the essential duties of his authority, remaining primarily concerned with his own deification for almost two-thirds of his long reign. Is this decision made of free will, or is it necessitated by some disabling disease? Examination of his mummy reveals that at his death Ramses must have been practically paralyzed by anky-losis spondylitis, a disorder in which the vertebrae (bones of the spinal column) gradually fuse together.

HISTORY ACCORDING TO RAMSES: KADESH, 1274 B.C.

In year 5, Ramses II starts a campaign to reestablish control over the country of Amurru, located between the Egyptian and Hittite empires and source of the rivalry between the two powers. Ramses learns that the Hittite king Muwatallis has supposedly gathered 2,500 chariots and more than 35,000 soldiers to seize Amurru. If Ramses doesn't act fast, there is great danger that he will see the regions north of the Syrian coast fall into Hittite hands. He assembles four armies (named after the gods Ra, Amun, Ptah, and Seth) of 5,000 men each, hundreds of chariots, and sets off. The confrontation takes place at the foot of the town of Kadesh. Misled at first by false information, Ramses sets up camp without waiting for all his troops to arrive. His scouts capture two soldiers who inform him that the enemy army is nearby. In fact, the Hittite army attacks fiercely and quickly overruns the Egyptian fortifications. With the help of the god Amun, Ramses II pushes back his adversary, who is surprised by an Egyptian army attacking from the other side. The Hittites withdraw, but most of their army succeeds in retreating without being destroyed. The next day, Ramses II regroups all his troops and attacks the Hittites. He does not succeed. In fact, he retreats back toward Egypt, leaving his enemies in control of the land. Technically, Ramses II has lost the battle of Kadesh because he left the region in enemy hands. But the king of Upper and Lower Egypt is not allowed to lose, and his heroism during the first engagement allows him to transform the defeat into a splendid victory, which will be described on all the monuments of his reign.

**TWO HITTITE SPIES HAVE BEEN CAPTURED,
AND AFTER BEING BEATEN THEY CONFESS THAT THE HITTITE ARMY IS BEHIND THE FORTRESS.**
The two Hittite soldiers didn't want to speak, but our brave soldiers knew how to convince them to reveal the location of the enemy army. His Majesty then held a council and sent a messenger to hurry the arrival of the army of Ra.

RAMSES II SINGLE-HANDEDLY ATTACKS THE HITTITE ARMY AND FORCES THE CHARIOTS TO WITHDRAW.

His Majesty is surrounded by cowards, but then he stands up and like Montu puts on his armor and takes his weapons, while his faithful horseman harnesses the horses named "Victory-at-Thebes" and "Mut-is-satisfied." Like Baal and Seth, His Majesty rushes, alone, in the middle of 2,500 enemy chariots and makes them retreat with the help of his father Amun.

THE BATTLE HAS ENDED. THE KING, STANDING IN HIS CHARIOT, CONTEMPLATES HIS VICTORY. IN FRONT OF HIM THREE SCRIBES COUNT THE HANDS CUT OFF THE ENEMIES KILLED IN BATTLE. THE OFFICERS GREET HIS MAJESTY. THE ROYAL PRINCES LEAD AWAY THE PRISONERS.

The victory is complete! Standing on his chariot, His Majesty assists the counting of the hands cut from the enemies fallen in the battle. The royal princes drag away long lines of prisoners, while His Majesty's officers sing his courage.

THE EGYPTIAN ARMY NEEDS YOU

Great-grandson of a soldier, and a brave fighter himself, Ramses II certainly appreciates the value of military men. The biographies of some high-ranking officials of his administration clearly indicate that the military career was a good stepping stone on the way to more prestigious and peaceful duties. For example, a man named Souti, a high officer of the army and First Charioteer of His Majesty, seems to be particularly favored by Ramses II because he also holds the position of chief of treasury and is responsible for the building of the king's tomb.

At this time the army is divided into four large units, each under the protection of a god: Amun, Ra, Ptah, and Seth. Each unit contains around 5,000 soldiers and several hundred chariots. The chariots and horses are well attended, as indicated by this royal order: "Take care of the preparation of the warhorses of the squadron intended for Kharu [Syria], as well as of their chief of stables and stable hands—their bags filled with provisions and finely chopped straw, their knapsacks full with bread. Each donkey under the surveillance of two men. Their chariots . . . loaded with all kinds of weapons of war."

The chariot corps is by far the most prestigious unit in the army and is reserved for royal princes and the most valuable soldiers. The chariot, a foreign invention, was adopted by pharaohs at the beginning of the New Kingdom. Since then it has become the spearhead of the army. This light vehicle is drawn by two horses and mounted by two people, a driver and a fighter armed mainly with a bow and javelins. Although the status of a soldier is described in the golden legend of the New Kingdom as a source of enrichment and an opportunity for social promotion, reality must have been frequently quite harsh: "Come, let me describe to you the pains of the soldier, for his superiors are many: the general, the chief of archers, the *seket*-officer who is in front of them, the flag bearer, the lieutenant, the scribe, the leader of 50 men, the chief of the garrison . . . he must be awake from first light on. Something is always on his back as if he were a donkey, and he works till sunset . . . He is hungry, his body is tormented, he is dead while being still alive . . . Long are the marches on the hills. He drinks water every three days, a stinking liquid with a taste of salt. His body is exhausted by dysentery. . . . And they say: 'Come on, forward, valuable soldiers, go and win glory!' But he no longer knows where he is. His body is weak, his knees bend in front of the enemy. . . . If he escapes alive, he is exhausted by the marches. . . . If he runs away and goes with the deserters, his entire family is sent to prison. When he dies on the edge of the desert, there is no one to perpetuate the memory of his name. Both death and life are painful for him."

1 Ramses II in his war chariot
2 Egyptian foot soldiers of the XIX Dynasty.
3 Egyptian archer of the XIX Dynasty.

THE GREATEST EVENT IN MOTION PICTURE HISTORY!

Photographed by Karsh, Ottawa

PARAMOUNT PRESENTS

CECIL B. DeMILLE'S
PRODUCTION

THE TEN COMMANDMENTS

STARRING

CHARLTON HESTON · **YUL BRYNNER** · **ANNE BAXTER** · **EDWARD G. ROBINSON** · **YVONNE DE CARLO** · **DEBRA PAGET** · **JOHN DEREK**

SIR CEDRIC HARDWICKE · NINA FOCH · MARTHA SCOTT · JUDITH ANDERSON · VINCENT PRICE

DIRECTED BY CECIL B. DeMILLE

TECHNICOLOR®

WRITTEN FOR THE SCREEN BY AENEAS MacKENZIE · JESSE L. LASKY, Jr. · JACK GARISS · FREDRIC M. FRANK
Based upon the HOLY SCRIPTURES and other ancient and modern writings PRODUCED BY MOTION PICTURE ASSOCIATES, INC.

VISTAVISION

THE CROSSING OF THE RED SEA: NOT ENOUGH TO MAKE A MOVIE!

Moses versus Ramses II! With the flight from Egypt and the crossing of the Red Sea toward the Sinai and the Promised Land, one nation creates its foundation myth, while another seems consigned to a bizarre fate.

Today, some historians date the escape of the Jews from Egypt to the reign of Ramses II. However, the annals of the land of pharaohs make no reference to this event, possibly because Ramses II doesn't like to mention his failures!

In fact, the whole story of the relationship between Egypt and Jews is founded on a perfectly understandable difference of perspective. For the Egyptians, the valley of the Nile is the great power of the region, for the others—those nomads from the north (who were nothing more than one of many unimportant tribes to the Egyptians)—the Nile is a rich source of land, and potentially a good place to settle. The Jews presumably enter Egypt during the frequent Hyksos invasions around 1600 B.C. or are brought as captives by the great Egyptian conquerors of the XVIII Dynasty. To meet the demands of the building fervor of Ramses II, the Jews are forced to participate. The Old Testament recounts "They built for Pharaoh treasure cities, Pithom and Ramses" (Exodus 1:11), while texts from the time of Ramses mention the soldiers and the Apiru (possibly Jews) who drag the stones for building the temples.

If one accepts that the Exodus takes place during the reign of Ramses II, then when exactly does it occur? Could this event possibly correspond with the disappearance of the king's first prince-heir in the year 20 as part of the plagues sent by God as retribution upon Egypt: "the death of the first born of Egypt?"

A TREATY IS NOT NECESSARILY WRITTEN ON PAPER

Engraved in stone in the temple of Karnak and at the Ramesseum, one of the oldest treaties in history that has come directly to us puts an end to the conflict between Ramses II and the Hittite king Hattusil III. Having transformed his defeat at Kadesh into a victory, Ramses II cannot resist from presenting the treaty as yet another new victory:

"In the twentieth year of the reign, the first month of the season of *peret*, the twenty-first day . . . a royal messenger arrives . . . carrying a silver tablet given by the big chief of Hatti, Hattusil . . . in order to implore peace from His Majesty . . . the son of Ra, Ramses-beloved-by-Amun."

The clauses in the treaty are similar to ones we would see today and can be outlined under the following four major points:

1) The frontiers must be respected as they are defined (in a previous treaty, now lost).

2) Mutual military assistance in case of attack from a third party.

3) Mutual military assistance in case of rebellion of a vassal state.

4) Extradition of Egyptian or Hittite refugees who defect to the opposite side.

This treaty is, of course, guaranteed by the gods of the two countries, using very robust language to make it seem more binding: "A thousand deities from among the gods and goddesses of the country of the Hatti, and a thousand deities from among the gods and goddesses of the country of Egypt, are with me witnesses to these words."

This treaty of peace and friendship between the two sovereigns is reinforced by a royal marriage. In year 34 of his reign, Ramses II marries the daughter of a Hittite king. What remains from the correspondence between the two sovereigns is telling. The Hittite king proposes to Ramses II to marry his daughter. This will be a lucrative "acquisition," for as he writes to Ramses: "The dowry will be nicer than the one for the daughter of the king of Babylon." But the girl is delayed, and Ramses II complains of seeing neither the girl nor the dowry. This, in turn, brings a scathing answer from Hittite Queen Pudoukhepa: "You shouldn't be suspicious of us, but trust us . . . does my brother have no possessions? . . . it is neither friendly nor honorable . . . that you, my brother, want to become rich at my expense!"

Ultimately, all ends well: "Then he [the Hittite king] had his elder daughter sent with a magnificent tribute of gold, silver, bronze, slaves, horses without number, cattle, goats, and rams in the ten thousands . . ."

ADVERTISING: THE KEY TO

"Ramses II is the greatest pharaoh of Egypt!" Now, who might have said that? Why, Ramses, himself. After all, who would know better than he? Nobody. And the proof?

Egypt is the only country to possess two of the seven wonders of the ancient world—the huge pyramids of Giza and the lighthouse of Alexandria—but do you know the names of their builders?* And why not?—because they didn't advertise. On

the other hand, Egypt does have one of the greatest publicity experts in history: Ramses II. For although he has only his one victory at Kadesh—and even that has some of the bitterness of unadmitted defeat—Ramses styles himself a grand conqueror.

He does this by placing his name everywhere in the country, on the monuments built before his time and on all those he builds along the Nile valley, from the Delta to distant Nubia.

A SUCCESSFUL KINGSHIP

In front of his funeral temple, the Ramesseum, a granite statue is erected that is more than 55 feet high and weighs around a thousand tons. And although this statue is imposing, Ramses' most famous monument is the big temple of Abu Simbel, the facade of which measures 125 feet in width, 110 feet in height, and is cut into the cliff wall to a depth of nearly 200 feet. After you're overwhelmed by the sheer colossal dimensions of the four huge statues of the king dominating the entrance to the temple, you'll have no doubts of the divinity of Ramses II when you finally reach the inner sanctuary and come face to face with the king's image, this time deified among those of the greatest gods of Egypt.

* Khufu, Khephren, and Menkaure built the pyramids. Ptolemy I assigned the construction of the lighthouse to Sostratus of Cnidus, and it was finished under Ptolemy II.

31

THAT BABY WAS SO CUTE, I DECIDED TO HAVE

Ramses II fathers around 110 children, with nearly an equal number of boys and girls. Listing them is difficult, in particular since some of them change their name following the example of the first son (by queen Nefertari), who is at first called Amunherunemef, then Amunherkhopshef, and finally Sethherkhopshef. The mothers of some of the children are known, but most of the mothers remain anonymous. Many of Ramses' children are the offspring of the many royal mistresses who make up his harem. Because he lives so long, Ramses' elder sons die before they can succeed him. It is his thirteenth son, Merneptah, who finally ascends the throne on Ramses' death. Khaemwase, his fourth son, is the son we know best. Being considered the prince-heir, he serves as the high priest of Ptah at Memphis, where he reorganizes the tombs of the Apis bulls (today known as the Serapeum and in Saqqara). He must be well respected because he is entrusted to proclaim the first five *sed* feasts of his father across the entire country. Not much is known about the daughters, except for three of them who become royal spouses to their own father: Bint-Anath, Meryetamum, and Nebettawy. There is also his sister Henutmire (one of the Great Royal Wives). It is even possible that Bint-Anath has a child with her father.

RECENTLY

A team of American archeologists discovered a collective burial place in the Valley of Kings. The entrance of this tomb, known as number 5 of the valley, had been discovered in the nineteenth century but seemed to lead to a dead end. However, since February 1995 more than sixty rooms have been discovered, with inscriptions mentioning the names of many sons of Ramses II. At last, we'll have some names to go with all those numbers.

While the status of women is relatively favorable in Egypt, men still dominate society. Polygamy is allowed, but is exercised mainly by the men of the upper classes, who can afford it, since you have to treat all your various spouses equally. Father of countless children, Ramses II has many Great Royal Wives, some of whom are his own daughters, as well as a tremendous number of mistresses about whom we know nothing.

Hentmirê — — My sister

Nefertari — — My Great Royal Wife, for whose love the sun shines

Isisnofret — — My Great Royal Wife number two

Bentanat — — My daughter (born to Isisnofret)

Méritamon — — My daughter (born to Nefertari)

Nenettaouy — — My daughter

Maâthornéférourê — — Daughter of the great king of Hatti, Hattusil

Tell the attendant of my harem at Mi-wer to draw up today's list of concubines, with both Egyptian and foreign women.

OH, HOW I'VE LOVED YOU ALL

All these women are housed in the royal residences and harems at Thebes, Memphis, and Pi-Ramses, and also in a large harem at Mi-wer, south of the oasis of Fayum. It is not always easy to live together, and we know that Ramses III, the last important Ramses and the second king of the XX Dynasty, may have lost his life as a result of a plot hatched in the harem by one of the queens who wanted to push her son to the throne.

SEEN AT THE ROYAL COURT

This is year 21 of Ramses II's reign. The king is in his residence at Pi-Ramses and is preparing to receive the messenger of Hattusil III, king of Hatti, successor of his old adversary at Kadesh, Muwatallis. Threatened by the

WENNEFER, HIGH PRIEST OF AMUN
Before being named to the supreme priesthood of Amun, he holds the same function for the cult of the god Osiris at Abydos. This is a typical example of how the big families of the kingdom retain their influence by holding both priestly and civilian functions—his brother will be a vizier of Ramses II, while his daughter will marry another high priest.

SETHHERKHOPSHEF, PRINCE-HEIR
First son of Ramses II, by Nefertari, he is first called Amunherunemef and later Amunherkhopshef. He does not survive the long reign of his father.

KHAEMWASE, FOURTH SON OF RAMSES II
Isisnofret gives birth to this high priest of Ptah at Memphis. One of the most interesting personalities of the reign, his interest in Egypt's past and his determination to restore the monuments of the glorious ancestors win him the name "archaeological prince." Much later, during the Ptolemaic Period, Khaemwase will be the subject of wonderful stories that present him as a great magician.

TUYA, THE QUEEN MOTHER
Sixty years old when the peace treaty is accepted, she probably dies soon after.

advance of the Assyrians toward his eastern borders, the Hittite king would like to make peace with Egypt. Ramses II has gathered his highest officials in the palace's great audience hall, guarded by his royal mercenaries.

HEQANAKHT, VICEROY OF NUBIA
He is responsible for the entire region extending south of Aswan, where he must maintain order and assure the exploitation of the gold mines.

PASER, VIZIER
He is already an old man, the son of a high priest of Amun, he was the vizier of Seti I and crowned Ramses II.

PANEHESI (HIS NAME MEANS "THE NUBIAN"), CHIEF OF TREASURY
He holds a position similar to that of secretary of the treasury, but has no great power and answers to the orders of the king and the vizier.

SETAU, FIRST SCRIBE
Only at the beginning of his career in the Egyptian administration, he will eventually gain the title of viceroy of Nubia.

URHIYA, GENERAL
Of foreign origin, he starts his military career under Seti I and continues it under Ramses II. His career will lead him to be named high steward of the Ramesseum, the king's funeral temple.

WHAT'S ON THE AGENDA?

The Egyptian year has 365 days divided into twelve months of thirty days, added to which are five supplementary days. These twelve months are grouped in three seasons: the flood (*akhet*, from July to October), the winter or season of sowing (*peret*, from November to February), and the summer or season of harvests (*shemu*, from March to June). The numbering of years is renewed at the beginning of each reign. A precise date would be expressed in the following way: "the 21st year, the first month of *peret*, the 21st day of reign of His Majesty king of Upper and Lower Egypt . . . the son of Ra, Ramses-loved-by Amun" (this is the date of the peace treaty with the Hittites). Individual days are divided into twenty-four hours, twelve for the day and twelve for the night.

2nd month, season of shemu
Day 12, Ramses II

DAY

2nd hour Wake up, wash, and dress

3rd hour Ritual bath, purification, and sacrifice to gods

4th hour Read the mail

5th hour Receive the chief of the scribes

land surveyors of the royal estate

7th hour Go see Nefertari in the harem, lunch, nap

11th hour Official reception for foreign ambassadors (summon the Superintendent of the Mouths of Nile)

NIGHT

2nd hour Banquet with the ambassadors—

It is very probable that the awakening of the king involves a ceremony to which the barber and other servants are invited as well as members of the royal family and high officials.

3RD HOUR (8:00 O'CLOCK)
Sacrifices to the gods are essential for cosmic equilibrium, and the gods' earthly representative is the pharaoh. His first concern after having washed is therefore to carry out these rituals, probably in a chapel in the interior of the palace.

4TH HOUR (9:00 O'CLOCK)
In such a bureaucratic country the reading of the reports of various officials must be one of the king's main activities.

5TH HOUR (10:00 O'CLOCK)
The economy of the country relies primarily upon agriculture. The land surveyors have an important role because taxes are determined based on their information.

7TH HOUR (NOON)
Nefertari is certainly the preferred royal spouse of Ramses II. One can imagine, therefore, that she is always in the harem of his residence. At this time of the day, when it is particularly hot, there is nothing better to do than to rest sheltered from the sun.

11TH HOUR (4:00 O'CLOCK IN THE AFTERNOON)
The reception of foreign ambassadors is one of the favorite occupations of the pharaohs, who see in it a renewed proclamation of their dominion over the world. For instance, the Superintendent of the Mouths of the Nile is a high official, frequently of military origin, responsible mainly for the northern borders of the country.

nd month, season of shemu
Day 13, Ramses II

DAY

TH HOUR REPORT ON PROGRESS OF THE
ILDING OF MY "HOUSE FOR ETERNITY"
5TH HOUR JUSTICE MEETING
TH HOUR WILD BULL HUNT WITH THE
ROYAL SONS

DAY 13
4TH HOUR (9:00 O'CLOCK)
The construction of his tomb is the king's main concern. Believe it or not, despite his sixty-year reign the tomb of Ramses II in the Valley of the Kings is not finished at his death (possibly because he has had it remodeled several times).

5TH HOUR (10:00 O'CLOCK)
Justice, represented by the goddess Maat, is an essential element in cosmic equilibrium. The gods are believed to nourish themselves on truth and justice, and the pharaoh is a guarantor of justice.

11TH HOUR (4:00 O'CLOCK IN THE AFTERNOON)
Hunting is one of the favorite sports of the pharaohs. Hunting the wild bull that lives at the borders of the valley is also symbolic of the fight against the forces of evil.

SO MANY GODS, SO LITTLE TIME!

One god, three gods, hundreds of gods, gods of yesterday and the day before yesterday, falcon-god, crocodile-god, ibis-god, baboon-god, cat-god, lioness-god, and so on—these are the gods of a people who have never denied those of their ancestors (until the advent of the face of the sun disk, the exclusive cult imposed by the fanatic ruler Akhenaton). Egyptian polytheism is the result of a history that takes place in a well-defined geographical zone—the Nile valley between Aswan and the Mediterranean; it is the result of popular beliefs enriched by the ceremonies practiced in the temples to honor the great glory of the gods as well as the pharaohs. Here are some of the actors in this polytheistic theater:

1—THE THEBAN TRIAD
Amun, his wife the goddess Mut, and the child-god Khonsu.

2—THE MEMPHITE TRIAD
The god Ptah, the lioness goddess Sekhmet, and the child-god Nefertum (missing in the picture).

3—THE THREE STATES OF THE SUN
Khepri, the beetle, symbolizes the rising sun ("becoming"); falcon-headed Ra is the sun at its zenith ("being"); while Atum represents the setting sun.

4—THE GODDESS MAAT
Daughter of Ra, she symbolizes the order, justice, and cosmic equilibrium that allow the world to exist out of chaos.

5—THE ELEPHANTINE TRIAD
The ram-headed god Khnum flanked by his consort Satis and his daughter Anukis.

6—THOTH
The ibis-headed god, protector of scribes, is sometimes depicted as a baboon or an ibis.

7—TAWERET
The hippopotamus goddess who protects pregnant women.

8—SOBEK AND HAROERIS ("HORUS THE ELDER")
The crocodile-god and the falcon-god, joint masters of the temple of Kom Ombo in Upper Egypt.

9—MONTU
The falcon-headed warrior-god, patron of the city of Thebes before being overshadowed by Amun.

OSIRIS AND ISIS
Don't look for them—they're not in this family album. The god of the dead and his sister-wife cut out of this reunion!

A NUCLEAR PLANT IN THE MIDDLE OF THE CITY

"Thus the Egyptian temple is not a house of prayer, where people come to look for the tranquility of the soul . . . because the general populace does not enter the sanctuary. . . . The temple is rather a kind of factory as rigorous in the selection of its personnel as it is closed to the outside world, a facility as dangerous to maintain as a nuclear plant might be for us today."

This definition, given by the Egyptologist Serge Sauneron, captures the difference between an Egyptian temple and one of our modern places of worship. The temple is the house of the god, and any activity performed by those who serve there—the priests are called "servants of god"—is designed to ensure the proper upkeep of the god and his house. The comparison to a nuclear power plant is also appropriate because of the extraordinary energy perceived to emanate from the gods within the temple. It is this energy that allows for the preservation of the ordered universe so that it will not revert to its original state of chaos, and it also keeps at bay the evil powers that continuously threaten to plunge all existence back into chaos.

The fundamental element of the temple, the most mysterious one, is a small locked chapel that holds the *naos*, a shrine containing the statue of a god. All around it are other rooms that serve as small chapels dedicated to associated gods as well as areas where the objects necessary for worship are stored. In front is a series of gradually larger and higher rooms, known as hypostyle halls, with ceilings supported by rows of columns. Beyond these is a peristyle, a courtyard open to the sky and usually enclosed by a series of columns that support a roof over a gallery. Finally, there is a monumental gateway composed of an entrance framed by a pair of stone blocks: the pylon. All around the temple are groups of secondary structures, administrative buildings, houses for the priests, a well, and a sacred lake. A brick wall isolates this micro-city from the outside world. Many Egyptian temples are relatively simple buildings, but the temple of Karnak that shelters Amun, the great god of the New Kingdom, has been the object of great attention from the pharaohs who, one after the other over a period of nearly 1,500 years, have added obelisks, halls, courts, and pylons, of which there are no fewer than ten.

THE OPULENCE OF GODS EQUALS THE OPULENCE OF PRIESTS

"Did I not build for you many huge monuments, and have I not filled your temple with prisoners? . . . It is for you that I have gathered these lands to nourish your holy offerings. I arranged that tens of thousands of oxen were brought to you. . . . It is for you that the boats sail on the Great Green [Mediterranean Sea] in order to bring you tribute from foreign countries."

This is the speech Ramses II makes to Amun during the moment of distress when his army is being pushed back by Hittite chariots in front of Kadesh. Ramses, who has done so much for his god, is desperate, having not received any divine help from his protector. The gods of Egypt do watch over the country, but in exchange the king must bring them food, incense, and riches of all kinds. The pharaohs of the New Kingdom, including Ramses II, are great builders. Most of their efforts are directed toward erecting structures for the gods. A great many priests are needed to populate these countless and occasionally gigantic temples, and kings need a great deal of wealth to maintain all the priests. Famous soldier and great builder, Ramses II seems to have been particularly generous. We can get an idea of the extent of this generosity from an inventory of the donations made by his most noted successor, Ramses III. A papyrus written just after his death lists all the donations this pharaoh made to the country's temples during his reign of 31 years (not even half as long as the reign of Ramses II):

	Goods donated	Portion for Amun of Thebes
Men and women	107,615	86,486
Head of cattle	490,386	421,362
Vineyards and orchards	513	433
Boats and ships	88	83
Towns	169	65
Land	1,071,780 aroures*	864,168 aroures

(* An aroure is a measurement of land equal to about 2,756 square yards.)

In addition to these there are more donations, including 2,756 statues the king ordered to be built for the estate of Amun, which cost 18,252 deben of gold and silver (weighing roughly 4,500 pounds) and the same quantity of semiprecious stones, as well as 112,132 deben of copper, lead, and tin (nearly 5,000 pounds).

To finish this short summary of the wealth of Amun, remember that each year Ramses III allotted to him 289,530 aquatic birds and nearly 100,000 bags of grain (some 3,680 tons) on top of what already existed in the coffers.

The wealth of the gods naturally makes the priests rich, enabling them to possess great economic power. The pharaoh seeks to control this power through his nomination of high priests. However, this power can present a threat if royal power weakens, as will happen to the distant descendants of Ramses II at the end of the XX Dynasty.

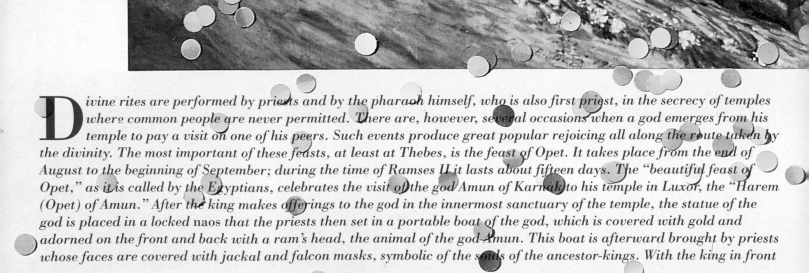

Divine rites are performed by priests and by the pharaoh himself, who is also first priest, in the secrecy of temples where common people are never permitted. There are, however, several occasions when a god emerges from his temple to pay a visit on one of his peers. Such events produce great popular rejoicing all along the route taken by the divinity. The most important of these feasts, at least at Thebes, is the feast of Opet. It takes place from the end of August to the beginning of September; during the time of Ramses II it lasts about fifteen days. The "beautiful feast of Opet," as it is called by the Egyptians, celebrates the visit of the god Amun of Karnak to his temple in Luxor, the "Harem (Opet) of Amun." After the king makes offerings to the god in the innermost sanctuary of the temple, the statue of the god is placed in a locked naos that the priests then set in a portable boat of the god, which is covered with gold and adorned on the front and back with a ram's head, the animal of the god Amun. This boat is afterward brought by priests whose faces are covered with jackal and falcon masks, symbolic of the souls of the ancestor-kings. With the king in front

COME THE GODS

and with incense-bearing priests, the boat heads to the river joined by those of Mut, consort of Amun, and of Khonsu, their son. Surrounded by musicians and dancers the boats reach the Nile, where they are transferred to larger ships. These ships are then hauled from the bank to the wharf in front of the temple of Luxor. Crowds along the riverbank applaud the dancers and singers accompanying the procession, which is followed by armed soldiers, men carrying banners, and chariots. When the destination is reached, the portable ships are unloaded and brought into the temple of Luxor, passing along a series of small kiosks that shelter tables laden with offerings. Afterward, the procession enters the "Harem of Amun," where the gods of Karnak remain for some twelve days. Although the people don't participate in these ceremonies directly and remain spectators throughout, they vividly express their joy at seeing so much pomp displayed outside the sacred temple. And during the processions and the god's stay in Luxor, beer flows liberally in the taverns of the town and free distributions of meat liven up everyone's daily existence.

THE SCRIBE, AN IDEAL SON-IN-LAW

"Become a scribe and love being one,
so that your name will live forever.
A book is better than a painted stela,
better than a well-built wall,
building, temple, or pyramid
in the hearts of those who pronounce their names.
In fact, a name in the mouths of people
is useful in the cemetery!
For when a man has disappeared, his body in the ground,
all his contemporaries transformed to dust,
the written work will put his memory
in the mouth of another who in turn will convey it to another."

For the Egyptians, whose foremost concern is eternity, what could be more attractive than the profession of scribe? It must be said that the statement above is the work of a scribe, meant to be read by another scribe. It's a kind of propaganda poster, also pointing out the prospect of enjoying one's earthy life as well: "Be a scribe! You will thus avoid all harassing work and be exempted from any type of labor. You will handle neither the hoe nor the pick, and you'll never carry a basket. You'll never touch an oar, and you'll be spared submission to an infinite number of masters and chiefs . . . for it is the scribe who supervises all work upon this earth."

The superintendent responsible for the House for Eternity of His Majesty is looking for a skilled scribe to fill the position of Royal Scribe in the Place of Truth.* Monthly wages of 14 deben in grain and other incentives in goods.

* The royal tomb and its offices.

48

The Superintendent of the estate of the Temple for the Millions of Years of the King-of-Upper-and-Lower-Egypt-Usermaatre Setepenre in the property of Amun* is seeking a beginner scribe, send a hand-written letter in hieroglyphs and hieratic. Previous experience preferred.

* Official name of the funerary temple of Ramses II, the Ramesseum

"You see, I teach you . . . to skillfully hold the palette in order to make you a royal adviser, so that the treasures and granaries open in front of you . . . so that you'll be dressed in fine linen clothing, possess horses, your own boat on the river, and subordinates who attend to you and serve you . . . so that they will build a villa in the city for you . . . Open your heart to the art of the scribe, protect yourself from all exhausting duties and become a respected person of distinction."

There is a downside to the profession—the training. But how difficult are the hardships of apprenticeship compared to the advantages of the situation? Four or five years of studies for learning the rudiments of reading and writing . . . years of blind obedience to a master, whose

The intendant of Paser, prince of the town and vizier, is looking for a scribe to keep the accounts of the estate of the prince of the town and vizier in the nome [province] of the town of the "White Wall." *
Experience a must.

* Memphis, the place of origin of Paser's family on his mother's side.

preferred teaching tool is the stick: "Do not delight in being lazy or you will be beaten. The ear of the boy is indeed in his back and only blows oblige him to be attentive." After spending your teen years in apprenticeship to learn the basic formulas, and then undertaking an internship with an active official, there's a final exam that consists of writing an essay in the style of the *Satire of the Professions*, a literary work that hails the scribe's profession and denounces the thanklessness of any other activity. At the end of these long studies, as a novice scribe, you will be justly proud of yourself and cannot help but be convinced of your superiority over everybody around you. Now you are ready to take your rightful position in the society of the living before tasting the fruits of eternity.

Writing is invented in the valley of Nile around 3000 B.C. The last known hieroglyphic inscription dates to the month of August A.D. 394. In between, for practical reasons, the Egyptians invent two other systems of writing, the hieratic and the demotic, which are nothing more than cursive simplifications of hieroglyphs. At first, these signs had an ideographic significance, indicating either an object or a living being or representing an action; thus the image of a fish signified a fish, that of a man drinking meant "to drink." The scribes then advanced to the phonetic stage: signs evoked not only a single image but also a sound. From then on, the sign for a mouth—which is called er—denotes a mouth but can also be used in any word to write the sound "r," just as the sign for hoe—pronounced *mer*—can be employed to write the sound "mer."

In this way the scribes invent 150 sound-signs, 24 of which have the value of a single letter and are grouped in an "alphabet." In order to facilitate reading, scribes put together ideographic and phonetic signs: the offering table may be written by its ideographical sign, which is read "htp," but quite frequently the scribe also adds the two phonetic signs "t" and "p," which make the reading more precise. But two words can be written in the same way and have different meanings; to distinguish them the scribe adds a sign that is not pronounced, called a determinative. Thus the group "nfr" means "beautiful" without a determinative, but when the hieroglyph for woman is added, it takes on the meaning of "young woman." In this way, the hieroglyphic system is at the same time both ideographic and phonetic. And now you can see why so much training was needed to become a scribe.

A FRENCH GRADUATE STUDENT ANSWERS THE $64,000 QUESTION

On September 22, 1822, Jean-François Champollion announces the greatest breakthrough in the mystery of deciphering hieroglyphic writing. Born in 1790 in Figeac, Jean-François Champollion leaves for Grenoble in 1801 to stay with his elder brother. By the age of eleven he already knows Greek and Latin and is studying Hebrew. In 1802, Jean-Baptiste Fourier, a famous mathematician and physicist who participated in Napoleon Bonaparte's Egyptian expedition, moves to Grenoble; he notices the young Champollion and introduces him to Egypt and hieroglyphics, which no one can yet decipher. The boy is enchanted and declares that one day he will find the way.

To do so, he learns all there is to know about Egypt: the discussions of classical authors on hieroglyphs, both Arabic and Coptic, which is the last variant of the language used by the pharaohs. His

discovery in 1822 is the fruit of a massive accumulation of knowledge as well as good fortune. "I've got it!" Champollion announces to his brother on September 14, 1822, before he collapses. His discovery has been made possible by the discovery in 1799 of a stone slab inscribed with the same text written in three systems of writing, two Egyptian (hieroglyphic and demotic) and one Greek. (Found in the town of Rosetta on the Nile, it is known as the Rosetta stone.) Champollion identifies signs representing the names of Ptolemy, Arsinoe, and Alexander. Other hieroglyphic inscriptions from the Greco-Roman period confirm his discoveries. But the real mystery is unraveled when he deciphers the royal names of the Pharaonic period, namely those of Ramses and Thutmosis. His passion soon exhausts him, and after his only voyage to Egypt, Jean-François Champollion dies in Paris on March 4, 1832.

The books of the ancient Egyptians look nothing like our books today, hardcover or paperback. The literature of Pharaonic Egypt has survived to the present day through a variety of means: scrolls and fragments of papyrus, potsherds, pieces of limestone (known as ostraca), and on the walls of temples and tombs. Starting with this collection of fragments, today scattered over the entire globe, we can reconstruct an outline of Egyptian literature, with its great classics, the commentaries on the pharaohs and other illustrious people, its "scientific" works, and the anthologies of mythological and religious texts.

1—Love Songs
This new genre, the poetry of love, flourishes during the New Kingdom, particularly the XIX Dynasty. These poems are intended for recitation at banquets, with suitable musical accompaniment.
2—The Lives of Illustrious People
The ancient Egyptians have a special fondness for autobiographies. The retelling of life's glorious achievements is frequently a "passport" to eternity.
3—Anthology of Modern Literature
The Ramesside period is a creative period in the literary field. *The History of the Predestinated Prince*, *The Story of the Two Brothers*, and *The Story of Truth and Lies* are leading examples.

LIST FOR CENTURIES

THUTMOSIS III: ANNALS

PENTAUR: KADESH

THE SATIRE OF THE PROFESSIONS

THE BOOK OF THAT WHICH IS IN THE UNDERWORLD

4—Great Classics of Literature
Various Egyptian novels can be considered "best-sellers." They are written during the Middle Kingdom and copied by young scribes of the New Kingdom. The main ones are *The Story of Sinhoue, The Story of the Shipwrecked, The Story of Oasien*, and the tales from the Westcar Papyrus.

5—Hymns to the Sun
Among the religious texts are a number of hymns dedicated to the sun god that are genuinely poetic. The king Akhenaton's fervor for his god of the solar disk, Aton, is most often mentioned, but other reigns during the New Kingdom, such as those of Amunophis II and Ramses II, produce highly lyrical works as well.

6—Thutmosis III: Annals
Engraved on the wall encircling the sanctuary of the ship in the temple of Karnak, this story describes the 17 military campaigns of King Thutmosis III. The text mentions that the inscription is based on the diary preserved in the royal archives. One can imagine that this diary was consulted by generations of scribes as a type of model for this genre of literature.

7—Pentaur: Kadesh
This text, reproduced on papyrus and engraved on the walls of Ramses II's temples, is a wonderful example of royal propaganda in epic form describing the king's victory at Kadesh. The most interesting point is that the author gives his name, dates his work (May 1270), and cites his sources: the royal archives.

8—The Satire of the Professions
The "bible" for all scribes. It emphasizes the value of the profession to which they have dedicated themselves by criticizing, sometimes ferociously, all other activities.

9—The Book of That Which Is in the Underworld
This is the Egyptian name for what we call today the *Book of the Dead*. This anthology of formulas is intended to allow the deceased to benefit continuously from the light of the sun god in order to avoid traps in the underworld. At times specially commissioned, this book is also mass produced, with the buyer needing only to add his name in the blank spaces provided.

Proportion is well observed

Any particular reason for showing the soles of all these feet?

WHAT'S MY BEST SIDE?

The Egyptians leave few walls in their temples and tombs undecorated. But this is not art for art's sake: in Egypt, artists are craftsmen who are expected to do their work well. And this means above all making every image into a representation of reality. To accomplish this, artists rely on a set of rules, rules that remain constant during all of Egypt's history.

These rules can be summarized in the following three points:

1) All the characteristics of a subject must be presented. Each of these characteristics must be given in its real dimensions and be presented in the shape that is most easily recognizable.
2) The various elements of a composition must be presented in relation to a moving viewer.
3) In any composition, the main subject must be larger than any secondary ones.

Without doubt, the first of these points is the most readily apparent since it brings us to what can be called the "false profile," a distinctive feature of Egyptian art

This is a profile?

Very good technique, nice pencil lines, but stop trying to be so original!

A-

that is particularly noticeable in human representations. The head, chest, and limbs of people are shown in profile, while the eyes, shoulders, and belly are depicted from a frontal viewpoint.

The second point relates to the custom of presenting a succession of scenes along a wall, forcing the viewer to move in order to understand the scenes much as we look across the panels in a comic book.

The third point is especially visible in, for example, representations of the battle of Kadesh. The main subject is not the battle itself, but the heroic conduct of

Ramses II during the fight, and he is always presented as being larger than anyone or anything around him.

Finally one should emphasize that the artist doesn't just throw his drawings "blindly" onto a surface. Each image is carefully prepared using a grid that permits the artist to follow the time-honored proportions.

In this grid a standing person occupies 19 squares, with one square for the hair, two for the forehead down to the base of the neck, ten for the base of the neck to the knees, and the final six for the knees down to the soles of the feet.

IF A MAN ███ HIMSELF
IN A DREAM . .

with his mouth full of earth, GOOD, it means he's eating (the goods) of his fellow citizens.

seeing a dwarf, BAD, it means half his life will be wasted.

seeing himself in mourning, GOOD, it means increasing his wealth.

seeing his face in a mirror, BAD, it means a new life.

diving in a river, GOOD, it means forgiveness for all evils.

Long before modern psychologists, the Egyptians express great interest in dreams. Their interest is easy to understand since they believe that while they're asleep at night they leave the earthly world. To them, dreams are awakenings into a different universe that allow them to foresee the future. Understanding dreams is therefore of the utmost importance, and

58

chewing
cucumber,
BAD,
it means turmoil is
coming ahead.

facing a leopard,
GOOD,
it means acting as a
leader.

sitting in a
vineyard in the
sun,
GOOD,
it means pleasure.

breaking a vase with
his feet,
BAD,
it means fighting.

the Egyptians interpret them with the aid of anthologies entitled *Keys to Dreams*. The most important of these collections is compiled during the time of Ramses, presumably using an earlier text, and it follows a simple formula: the phrase "If a man sees himself in a dream" followed by lists of dream descriptions, each interpreted and rated as either good or bad.

Egyptian medicine is very famous at the time of Ramses II. Correspondence with the Hittite king following the conclusion of peace between the two sovereigns bears proof of this. When one of Hattusil's vassals is sick, he makes inquiries of Ramses, who answers:

"I summoned an erudite doctor. [Doctor] Pariamakhu will be sent to prepare the herbs for Kurunta, king of the lands of Tarhuntas; he requires a [selection] of all the herbs appropriate for the symptoms you wrote to me about."

Once in a while an extremely difficult case is presented that requires Ramses to act as a diplomatic and gracious ruler:

"Come on now, as concerns Marazani, the sister of my brother, I, the king and your brother, know of her. Is she fifty? Not at all! She's sixty, it's obvious! Nobody can prepare medicines that would allow her to have children. But, naturally, should the God of the Sun and the God of the Tempest wish it, well, I'll send a good doctor and also a capable one, and they'll prepare for her some drugs for procreation."

As famous as it is, Egyptian medicine readily mixes magic with more normal medical practices. Chasing out the hostile powers that take possession of a patient's body is as important as prescribing the appropriate remedy:

"Incantation against the sickness 'meshpent': Go out, you who have entered, and do not take with you anything when leaving . . . run away from me, for I am Horus. . . . The magic formulas of my mother protect my body. . . . Go out! (seven times). Say this over the herb 'ennek'; bake the herb, grind it, and give it against this sickness."

Some magic formulas actually do not say anything intelligible at all: "Rakarabouna . . . raka . . . rakarabouna . . . estioumo . . ."

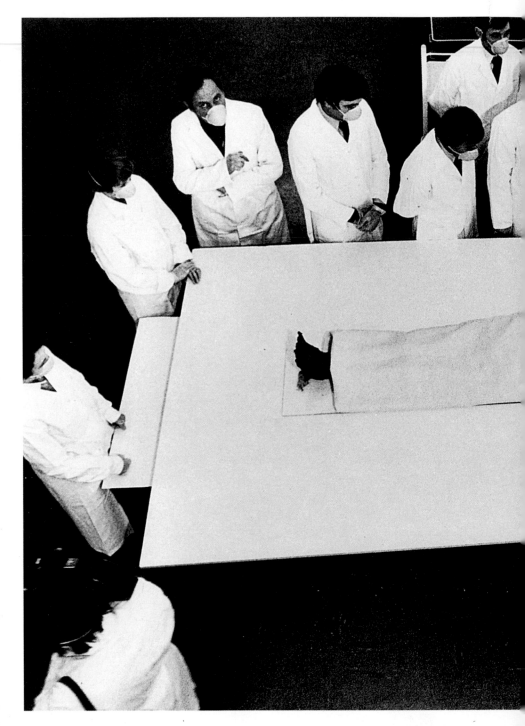

Even so, the fame of Egyptian doctors is based on real successes in fighting maladies. Such successes clearly result from careful observation of the human body as well as solid scientific understanding of the properties of the ingredients used as medicine. Naturally, there are limitations. Since they consider the heart as the body's vital organ, they conceive it as the meeting point for all bodily fluids: not just blood, but also tears, urine, and semen. And while they make efficient use of the properties of several herbs, some of their standard remedies include fly droppings or the excrement of pelicans and hippopotamuses.

All the same, Egyptian doctors sometimes adopt a surprisingly scien-

RAKA . . . RAKARABOUNA

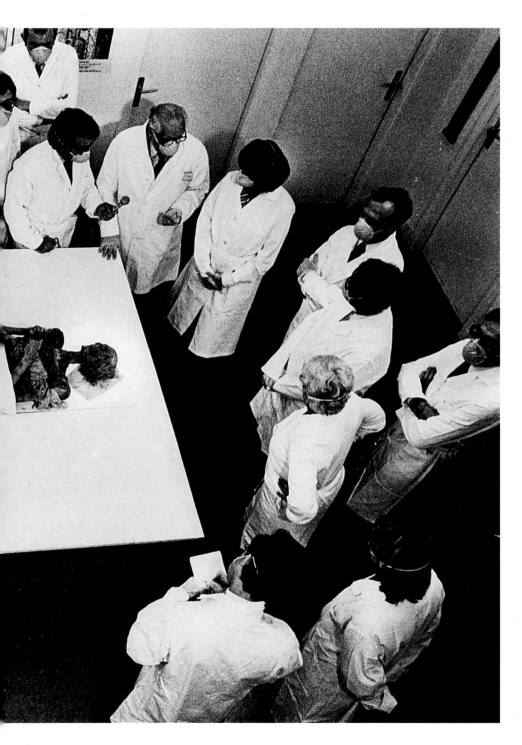

he is somebody who has an open wound in the head, penetrating to the bone and perforating the skull, and this is why he suffers neck stiffness. (4) It is a sickness that I shall treat. (5) Now, after you have sewn up the wound, you must lay fresh meat on it for the first day. You must not bandage the patient. Secure him to the securing-post until the wound starts to heal. Afterward you must treat the wound with fat, honey, and bindings every day." (6) Four comments follow, the most interesting of which is the last: "The sentence 'secure him to the securing-post' also means to place the patient on his usual diet without giving any prescription."

Of course, doctors sometimes find themselves facing illnesses they can't treat; the verdict here reads: "[This is] a sickness that cannot be treated."

SOME EGYPTIAN REMEDIES

To cure inflammation of the ear:
"Melilot [sweet clover]. Make an ointment with laudanum. Put it in the ears."

For a cough:
"Fresh colocynth. Put in a vase with water and drink for four days."

For constipation:
"Seeds of castor-oil plant. Chew and swallow with beer until all that is in your belly goes out."

To beautify facial skin:
"Powder of alabaster, 1 part; powder of natron, 1 part; salt of the North, 1 part; honey, 1 part. Mix all of these together and then use them as an ointment.

For headache:
"Stem of reed, 1 part; resin of the turpentine-tree, 1 part; juniper, 1 part; pitch, 1 part; berries of laurel, 1 part. Grind these and place on the head."

tific attitude, as indicated in a treatise on bone surgery written on a twelve-foot-long papyrus scroll. Each of the 48 cases reported in this papyrus is treated in a rigorous way: 1) case type; 2) examination of patient; 3) symptoms; 4) verdict; 5) treatment; 6) one or more comments. For example, the third case contains: "(1) Instructions concerning an open wound in the head, which penetrated to the bone and perforated the skull. (2) If you examine a person having an open wound in the head, penetrating to the bone and perforating the skull: you must palpate [feel] the wound; you will find him unable to look at his shoulders and his chest, his neck being painful and stiff. (3) You will say to your patient that

Do the Egyptians get help from extraterrestrial beings when erecting their huge monuments to honor their gods and deified kings? Such has been the opinion of various imaginative individuals. And, in truth, the colossal nature of some Egyptian architectural creations seems truly superhuman and has stimulated the imaginations of generations of dreamers (and crackpots). Still, you have to recognize an essential quality of the people of the Nile valley—their practical spirit and extraordinary capacity to use the resources of their environment in the most daunting of enterprises. The flooding of the Nile allows them to bring blocks of stone to building sites and frees the population from agricultural labors, making them available for construction projects. The surrounding cliffs supply limestone, sandstone, and granite, the soil of the valley is used in the making of bricks, and desert sand is employed in filling the cavities. When Ramses II decides to erect two obelisks in front of the Luxor temple, he has to rely on all the methods used by his predecessors. The workers first set up socles, stone pedestals on which the granite obelisks are to be placed. Then they build an enormous wall of bricks ❶ around these, leaving an opening to the top of the wall over each socle. Each opening is then filled with sand, but there are two openings at the bottom of the wall so that the sand can be removed later on. A long ramp,

TO BUILD IN STONE

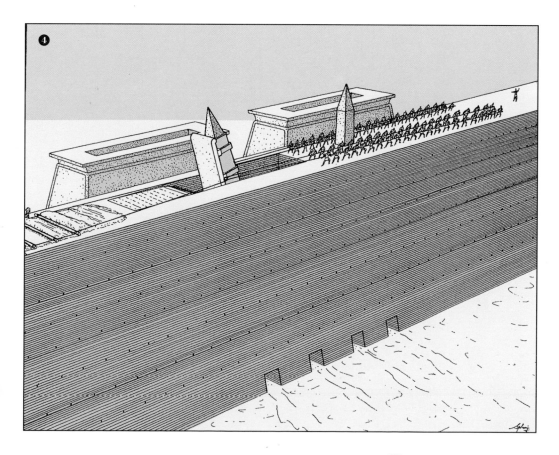

also made of bricks, provides for the transportation of the enormous obelisks, which are nearly 60 feet high and weigh 230 tons. The obelisks are set on skids, whose traction is facilitated by a slippery surface of silt kept continuously wet ❷. When the obelisks reach the top, they are placed over the sand-filled vertical cavities above the socles, and the sand is slowly removed, allowing the obelisks to drop steadily into the openings. When the cavity is empty, the obelisk is slightly tilted because one of the ridges of its base is blocked from fully descending by a slot provided when the socle was made. ❸ Now comes the most delicate stage: lifting the obelisk to the vertical position. ❹ The workers pull the top with ropes, in a movement countered on the bottom of the obelisk by the weight of heavy beams spread in a line on the sand. In this way the obelisk is slowly placed on its base without danger of breaking. And breaking such a piece would mean wasting all the hard work over a period of several months of those who made the obelisk, first extracting the blocks from the Aswan quarries, then cutting and polishing them, and then finally bringing these monoliths to the site. Once the erection process is finished, the huge brick wall is taken down, and the obelisks are celebrated. They are solar symbols, and the top is covered with gold that sparkles as though lit by thousands of fires.

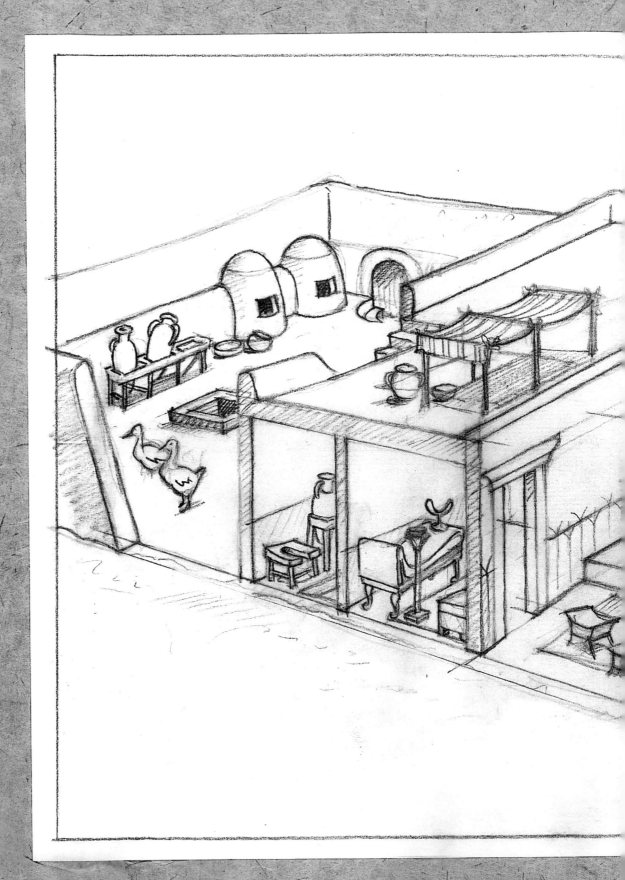

THREE ROOMS, BUT ALL THE COMFORTS OF HOME

The residences of the gods are made of stone, but those of mere mortals, including the pharaoh, are built with bricks made of mud dried in the sun. The basic layout is simple: an entrance, a reception hall with a ceiling higher than the rest of the house and drilled with holes that allow the passage of light and fresh air, and one or more private rooms with or

without bathrooms. The kitchens are outside. The furniture is pure basics: wooden chairs, mats, low tables, beds, storage chests. Food is stored in earthenware jars and willow baskets in the kitchen and the cellar. The Egyptians have guidelines for keeping things tidy: "Remedy for preventing mice from getting to things: eat lard. Smear it on everything." "The beginning of the treatment for chasing fleas out of the house: you will spray them with a solution of natron [naturally occurring sodium carbonate] until they vanish."

"THEY HARVEST WITH LESS LABOR

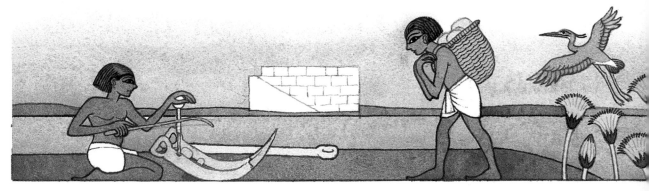

THE FLOOD SEASON

The valley is flooded. Only the hills on which the villages are built are spared. The peasants repair their tools, make rope, etc. The men are drafted to work on the vast building projects ordered by the king, building or enlarging temples everywhere in the country.

THE SOWING SEASON

First, the irrigation system must be readied. Next, the earth is plowed with the hoe or swing-plow, and finally the seeds are planted. Herds are led across the fields to bury the seeds in the earth.

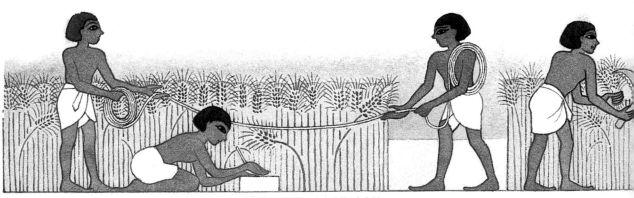

THE HARVEST SEASON

The wheat, barley, or flax is cut high using sickles made of wood, flint, or sometimes bronze. Afterward the wheat is brought to a threshing area to separate the grain from the chaff. Then the grain is winnowed to blow away the chaff. All this work is performed under the attentive eye of the scribe who determines the amount of tax to be paid.

Greeks like Herodotus, accustomed to the rocky soil of their motherland, are astonished by the generosity of Egyptian soil, which requires very little effort from those who work it. But let's allow those who live in this "country of abundance" to speak for themselves: "Let me remind you of the anxiety of the peasant when the civil servants come to estimate the tax on his harvest, after the serpents have taken half of the wheat and the hip-

THAN ANY PEOPLE IN THE WORLD"

—Herodotus, *The History*

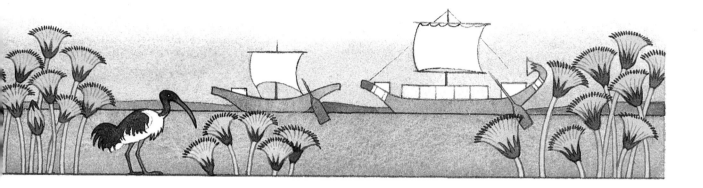

popotamus has eaten the rest. . . . The scraps of wheat left on the threshing floor have completely vanished, stolen by thieves. He cannot pay what he must for the oxen he has rented, and the oxen themselves are dead because of having plowed and pulled too much." "During the flood he is soaked from all sides, but he must maintain his equipment. . . . He spends his days repairing his tools and all his nights making rope."

FEMALE BREWER

Each home brews its own beer. The larger establishments (royal palace, temples) have a staff of employees whose main activity is taking care of the beer. Barley bread is crumbled in big earthenware jars, mixed with water, and left to ferment.

SMITHS

Two workers polish a large metal vase using tools made of stone.

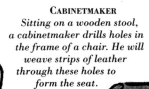

CABINETMAKER

Sitting on a wooden stool, a cabinetmaker drills holes in the frame of a chair. He will weave strips of leather through these holes to form the seat.

LEATHER TANNER

The tanner's trade is difficult, mainly because of the smell of the animal skins during curing. Here an artisan uses a stone blade to scrape hairs and fat off a hide. After this he'll put the skin in oil, then he will beat it, cure it, and make it soft again.

CARPENTER

He is using an adz with a copper blade and wooden handle to cut a tree trunk into planks.

BRICK MAKERS

Temples are made of stone, but the primary construction material is brick, made by mixing clay with straw, shaping the mixture in molds, and then drying the bricks in the sun.

SMITHS
They pour melted gold into molds in order to make small objects, such as amulets and pieces for inlay work in jewels and furniture.

ARTISTS
In a sculpture workshop, one worker carves the details of a lion statue with a bronze chisel and mallet, while another polishes the finished parts. A third worker paints a block-statue finished by the sculptors.

THEY USE THEIR ARMS TO FILL THEIR BELLIES

CARPENTERS
These carpenters are making a wooden boat. Two of them have copper chisels and mallets, two others have axes, and the last works with an adz.

PAINTER
He paints a piece of wooden furniture. He uses brushes made of plant fibers and paints made of minerals.

A young woman is grinding grain, the primary domestic task since bread constitutes the basic food of the Egyptians.

A smith chisels a metal vase. The shape of the vase is already formed, and now he must decorate it with words or drawings of gods.

THE PRICES OF LIFE

The Egyptians don't have coins until just before the Ptolemaic period. Until then, they barter, based on a unit of account called the deben, which is divided into 10 kites. The deben is a weight of about a quarter of an ounce; during exchanges it is most often related to a quantity of copper or, occasionally, a quantity of silver. During the time of Ramses II, the ratio of the value of copper to silver is 100 to 1.

The most consumed product is wheat, and the basic measure of wheat is the khar, equal to about 70 quarts. One khar of wheat is equal to two deben. The workers involved in building and decorating the royal tomb are housed together in a village at Deir el-Medina. This relatively privileged group leaves many archives that tell us the wages received by the workers as well as the value of various products expressed in deben.

The basic part of their payment consists of wheat to make bread, and barley to make beer. The monthly pay is as follows:

	Khar of wheat	Khar of barley	Value in deben
Crew chief:	5.50	2.00	15.00
Scribe:	5.32	2.00	14.64
Porter:	5.00	2.00	14.00
Doctor:	5.00	1.75	13.50
Worker:	4.0[1]	1.50	11.00
Guard:	3.25	1.25	9.00
Young man[2]:	1.50	0.50	4.00

In addition to these basic products there are bread, small cakes, and beer left over from offerings made to the gods and distributed after the gods have used their "energy," as well as vegetables, fish, drinks, and goods from gardeners, fishermen, and woodcutters associated with the village.

The situation of the workers of Deir el-Medina is envied by others. In fact, a man who wants to enroll his son there gives the two crew chiefs and the community scribe the following products: 1 leather bag valued at 15 deben; wood for an armchair, 30 deben; 1 folding stool and 1 plain stool, 30 deben. This total value is 75 deben, the equivalent of nearly seven months salary for a worker.

The price of the products that we know as well as the income of the workers of the royal tombs are not representative. The bulk of the population is composed of peasants who are tightly tied to the land on which they live and work. As for the privileged classes—the aristocrats, high officials, and priests of the richest temples—they have incomes that are difficult to estimate, and they keep servants and workers who supply them with all they need.

1. About two pounds of wheat per day to feed a family, without counting other goods distributed.
2. Probably an unmarried apprentice, which explains the low payment.

WOODEN CHEST:
3 DEBEN

BRONZE RAZOR:
2 DEBEN

PAPYRUS ROLL 12 FEET LONG:
2 DEBEN

IVORY COMB:
2 DEBEN

GRAIN BAG OF A KHAR
(ABOUT 70 QUARTS): 2 DEBEN

DONKEY:
25 DEBEN

CARPENTER'S AXE:
5 DEBEN

PAIR OF SANDALS:
2 DEBEN

BUNCH OF VEGETABLES:
1 DEBEN

GOOSE:
1/4 DEBEN

SARCOPHAGUS: 35 DEBEN, OF WHICH: WOOD
8, DECORATION 12, LABOR 15

FOLDING STOOL:
6 DEBEN

BASKET: 2 DEBEN

WINE JAR OF 4 1/2 QUARTS: 2 DEBEN

OX:
50 DEBEN

EXISTED

1 OSTRICH
Lives in the desert on the borders of the Nile valley. A fan of Tutankhamun is adorned by a representation of the king hunting ostriches from his chariot.

6 GOOSE
The goose is one of the sacred animals of the god Amun.

8 CLOCK
The Egyptians don't have clocks with wind-up mechanisms, but Egyptian priests use water clocks, or clepsydras.

9 DONKEY
At the time of Ramses the price of a donkey is about what a worker at the royal tomb earns in two months.

10 TOILETS
Affluent households have them. Holes are drilled in seats made of wood or stone, which are then placed above receptacles filled with sand.

11 BOOMERANG
The Egyptians use boomerangs to hunt the birds that flock in great numbers on the banks of the Nile.

12 OWL
The owl's appearance is so unmistakable from the front that it is never shown in profile, a truly rare exception to the conventions of Egyptian art.

BANANAS AND ORANGES
The Egyptians make do quite happily with dates, figs, pomegranates, and jujube fruits.

CHICKENS
The Egyptians have "hen houses," but they use them for wild birds caught along the banks of the Nile. Chickens finally appear around the time of Greek rule.

COINS
Minted coins first appear in Egypt only in the fourth century B.C. when the last Egyptian pharaohs began hiring Greek mercenaries who demand payment in currency.

DROMEDARY
The camel doesn't appear in the Nile valley until the age of the Ptolemies.

WHEELED TRANSPORT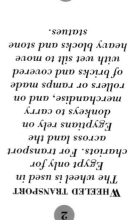
The wheel is used in Egypt only for chariots. For transport across land the Egyptians rely on donkeys to carry merchandise, and on rollers or ramps made of bricks and covered with wet silt to move heavy blocks and stone statues.

STYLISH DETAILS

A selection of interior-decorating ideas from the world of Ramses II.

These images, collected by Prisse d'Avennes in the nineteenth century, reproduce in color various elements of the architectural decoration of ancient Egypt, some of which, sadly enough, are no longer with us.

4 to 11. *Floral friezes decorating the walls of tombs that feature motifs of papyrus, lotus, grapes, and mandrake fruits.*

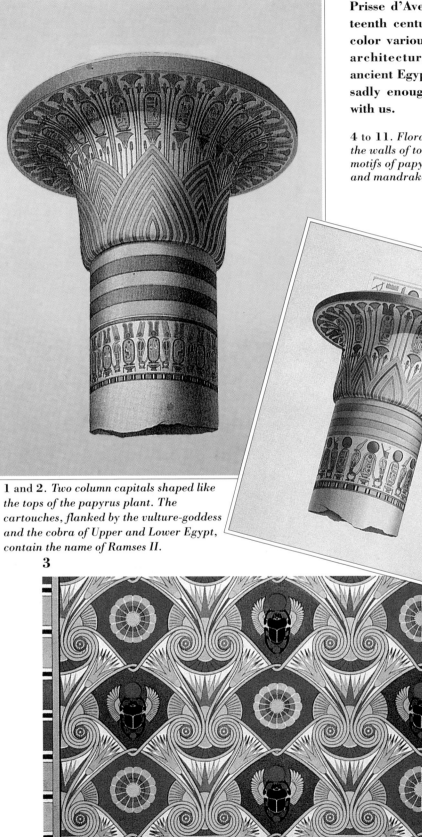

1 1 and 2. *Two column capitals shaped like the tops of the papyrus plant. The cartouches, flanked by the vulture-goddess and the cobra of Upper and Lower Egypt, contain the name of Ramses II.*

3

3. *Ceiling decoration. Winged scarabs and rosettes are framed by lotus and other motifs.*

4

5

6

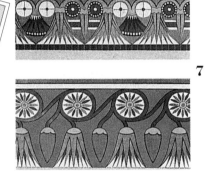

7

8

9

10

11

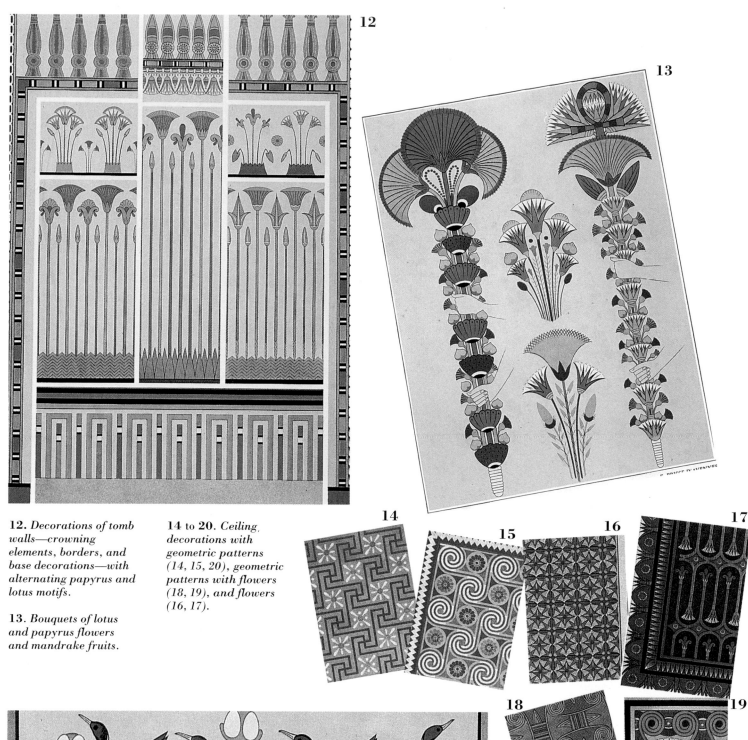

12. *Decorations of tomb walls—crowning elements, borders, and base decorations—with alternating papyrus and lotus motifs.*

13. *Bouquets of lotus and papyrus flowers and mandrake fruits.*

14 to **20.** *Ceiling decorations with geometric patterns (14, 15, 20), geometric patterns with flowers (18, 19), and flowers (16, 17).*

21. *Ceiling decoration with wild ducks taking off carrying their nests with eggs.*

75

THE DEAD SURE HAVE A GOOD APPETITE

"Thousands of loaves of bread, pitchers of beer, pieces of beef and poultry for the soul of . . ." These are items meant to feed the deceased, and the priests of the funerary cult had to provide them. The numerous pictures of offering tables loaded with all kinds of delicacies effectively demonstrate the importance of food to the ancient Egyptians. What could be more normal than this? After all, one must eat well to live! However, the banquet scenes painted on the tomb walls of the New Kingdom show that eating was a pleasure as well as a necessity.

The basis of the Egyptian diet is wheat, which is used in making bread. Ordinary bread is made in round loaves and baked without yeast on the outer walls of ovens. But sometimes bread is made with yeast and baked inside ovens or in conical earthen molds. For fun, or perhaps for magic purposes, bakers also make bread in various shapes, including those of animals and humans and even body parts. To make cakes the Egyptians add milk, honey, and dates to the dough. Besides wheat the peasants also grow barley, which is used to make beer, the most popular drink. The beer is full of impurities, however, and those who can afford it suck up their beer through a clay "straw" with a filter at its end.

The Egyptians eat various vegetables, too: onions are the most popular, but the Egyptians

also eat garlic, lettuce—famous for possessing aphrodisiac properties—cucumber, melon, chick peas, beans, and lentils. Fruits are reserved for those rich individuals who have gardens: figs, dates, carobs, berries, palm, and mandrake fruits are shown in offering scenes. Grape vines have existed in Egypt since the earliest times and are cultivated on trellises in the Delta and in the oases of the Libyan desert. Grapes are eaten as fruit and used to make a sweet juice, but their primary use is for wine. The grapes are pressed by feet, and the juice is then collected in earthenware jars and left to ferment. Later, the jars are sealed with a stopper made of straw covered with clay. Inscriptions on the jars give the source of the wine and the year of its vintage; the Egyptians may drink most of their wine while it is young, but they want it dated.

Fish from the Nile provide the most accessible source of protein for most of the population. Sold fresh, it is usually cut up, cleaned, and dried in the sun, which allows it to be preserved for longer periods. Birds are abundant in the swamps bordering the river. They are caught by professional hunters. Some are eaten grilled, but many are kept in farms for their eggs, especially such birds as geese and ducks, but also pigeons and even pelicans. In the Old Kingdom peasants stuffed geese (and hyenas!) for the preparation of paté. As for cattle, it is eaten only by the well-to-do and certain privileged categories of workers, such as those of the royal tombs. Such meat is usually grilled, but pieces of inferior quality are sometimes boiled.

YOU CAN DRESS RAMSES II !

Ramses II dresses very simply when not required to wear his royal crowns or carry his scepters. In fact, the warm climate of the country is conducive to wearing only light garments, made of fairly fine linen. Since time immemorial, the *shendjyt* has been the basic element of Egyptian garb, but the New Kingdom brings new fashions featuring nearly transparent tunics that fall in gracious folds over the arms. The pharaoh is distinguished from his subjects by the richness of his royal insignia, the symbols of his authority, as indicated by paintings in Thebes and the treasures found in the tomb of Tutankhamun.

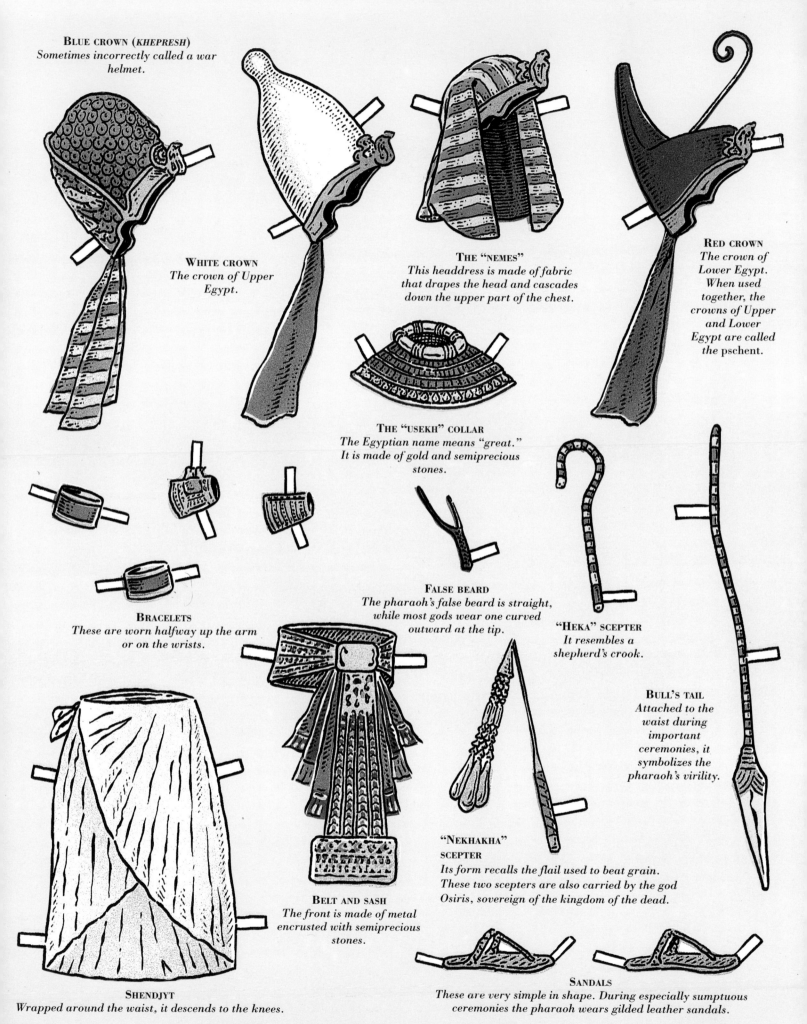

BLUE CROWN (KHEPRESH)
Sometimes incorrectly called a war helmet.

WHITE CROWN
The crown of Upper Egypt.

THE "NEMES"
This headdress is made of fabric that drapes the head and cascades down the upper part of the chest.

RED CROWN
The crown of Lower Egypt. When used together, the crowns of Upper and Lower Egypt are called the pschent.

THE "USEKH" COLLAR
The Egyptian name means "great." It is made of gold and semiprecious stones.

BRACELETS
These are worn halfway up the arm or on the wrists.

FALSE BEARD
The pharaoh's false beard is straight, while most gods wear one curved outward at the tip.

"HEKA" SCEPTER
It resembles a shepherd's crook.

BULL'S TAIL
Attached to the waist during important ceremonies, it symbolizes the pharaoh's virility.

"NEKHAKHA" SCEPTER
Its form recalls the flail used to beat grain. These two scepters are also carried by the god Osiris, sovereign of the kingdom of the dead.

BELT AND SASH
The front is made of metal encrusted with semiprecious stones.

SHENDJYT
Wrapped around the waist, it descends to the knees.

SANDALS
These are very simple in shape. During especially sumptuous ceremonies the pharaoh wears gilded leather sandals.

With its rectangular shape, this magnificent piece of jewelry resembles the front of a pylon, one of the massive stone gateways associated with Egyptian temples. The frame is made of gold inlaid with glass paste, and it surrounds a cartouche of Ramses II (similar to one on page 18) supported by a winged deity with a bull's head that is symbolic of the place where this piece was found, the Serapeum of Saqqara, burial place of the sacred bulls. At the bottom are the cobra and vulture symbolic of Lower and Upper Egypt with wings that arch upward to touch the royal cartouche. In the bottom corners are two djed pillars, Egyptian symbols of stability.

JEWELRY
IS NOT FOR WOMEN ONLY

Egyptian jewelry serves ornamental purposes much like today's jewelry.

Made of gold, silver, and semiprecious stones with vivid colors (or using glass paste and glazed pottery to imitate such stones), jewelry is part of the attire of both men and women who otherwise wear only clothes of white linen.

But jewelry also has great symbolic significance.

The two horses on the top of this ring are extremely unusual. Some scholars see them as representations of the two famous warhorses that carried Ramses II to his victory during the battle of Kadesh, which were named "Victory-at-Thebes" and "Mut-is-satisfied."

This significance rests primarily on the materials used: gold represents the flesh of the gods, the red of carnelian and red jasper is the color of blood and life energy, the green of turquoise and green jasper is equated with resurrection and joy, while the blue of lapis lazuli represents the protection of the sky. Of course, the motifs depicted are also symbolic, and many pieces of jewelry can be read like hieroglyphs, sometimes in a very simple fashion,

sometimes forming whole phrases.

WORDS AND INSTRUMENTS, BUT, SADLY, NO MUSIC

The walls of Egyptian tombs are painted with many images in which singers and musicians gather to delight the guests of banquets. But because the Egyptians use no system of musical notation, we know little today of what the music of Pharaonic times was like.

The most popular instrument is the harp, which is either set vertically on the ground or rested on the shoulder. During the New Kingdom the lyre makes its appearance. Flutes, oboes, and clarinets also appear, along with tambourines and wooden and ivory rattles and clappers. The trumpet is used in military fanfares. The sistrum, a kind of open bow from which hang small cymbals, is an instrument reserved mainly for religious ceremonies.

As for songs, we know only the lyrics, such as those from the "Harpist's Song," a popular tune of the New Kingdom that encouraged the listeners to rejoice in the present.

The dances that accompany these orchestras evolve over time: from highly acrobatic performances in the Old Kingdom, they gradually become more elegant during the New Kingdom and are probably very much like the belly-dancing practiced in the Near East today.

PLAYING TO PASS THE TIME OR TO JOIN ETERNITY?

"Play 'senet' sitting under the tent" is one of the ways the dead may come to life again, according to Chapter 17 of the *Book of the Dead*, that compendium of spells designed to insure safe passage to the other world. Nefertari, the favorite spouse of Ramses II, had herself shown this way in her tomb, sitting under a tent while playing the game alone against an invisible adversary "oblivion".

The Egyptians of the New Kingdom seem to have a special liking for two checkerboard games, the most widespread of which is the game of "senet." This game is played on a checkerboard table with 30 squares arranged in three parallel rows. Each of two players has an equal number of counters (ranging from five to seven) in two series of different shapes. The counters are moved with sticks or small bones.

The goal of the game is to get across the board with your counters following an S-shaped path while outrunning or blocking those of your adversary; the game is won when you get all your counters off the board. The fifteenth square and the last five squares bear images or hieroglyphic inscriptions

that denote a special status, either favorable or unfavorable, for the counter that lands on them. On the reverse of "senet" gameboards is another game, also quite popular, called the "game of 20 squares," whose rules seem different but reflect much the same gaming preferences. It is interesting to see the associations the Egyptians make between the world

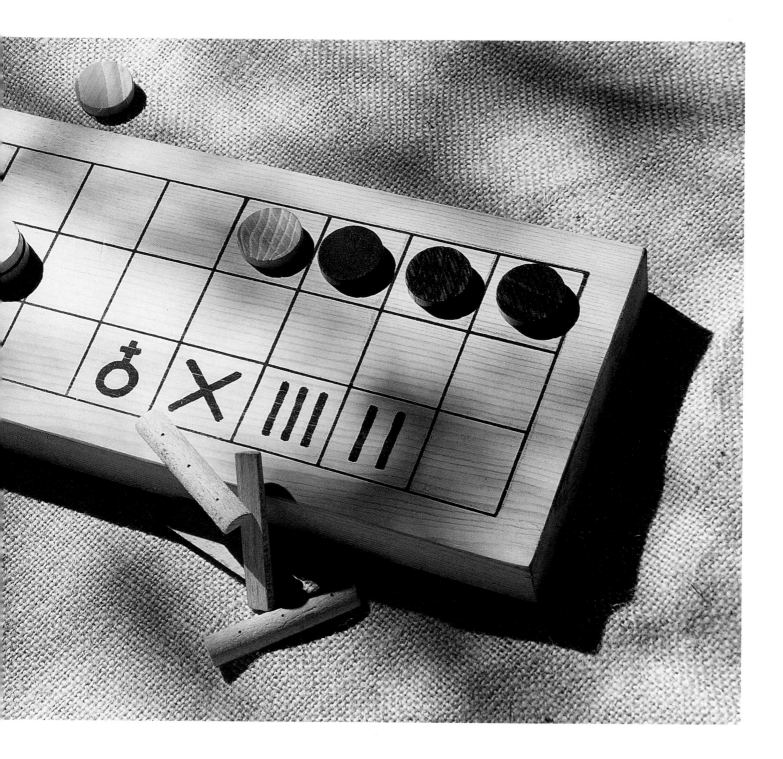

of the living and that of the dead. In Egyptian *senet* means "passing" or "overtaking," which denotes both the goal of the game, the overtaking of the adversary's counters, as well as the passing of one's own counters off the board. These notions are equally applicable in a funerary context, and the popularity of the game has presumably inspired one of the chapters in the *Book of the Dead*: winning the game allows the deceased to overcome any difficulties involved during his journey and to "pass" safe and sound into the next world.

For that very reason, the deceased brings his favorite game with him in his tomb, for it will help bring about his resurrection.

CALLING ALL BIRDS,
THERE'S A TRAITOR AMONG US!

"His Majesty set off against these wild bulls . . . the number caught by His Majesty when hunting

this day: 56." This text dates to the reign of Amunophis III, who ruled two centuries

before Ramses II, but hunting wild animals like bulls and lions has always

been one of the favorite sports of the pharaohs. When hunting, the pharaoh rides mounted in his chariot,

armed with a bow or javelins; this is both a pleasurable activity as well as physical exercise, and

on top of that it serves to symbolize the ever-renewed victory of the king against the enemies of Egypt.

While the big royal hunts have a very violent character, hunting is a more serene undertaking when practiced by the Egyptian aristocracy, for whom it is a favored pastime.

During the New Kingdom hunting is a family affair carried out

in the papyrus thickets that border the Nile. In a small boat, the

husband, accompanied by his wife and children, throws his boomerang

at birds, which fly off, scared by

this intrusion. Quite frequently the

hunter is also a fisherman, going after the river fish with a spear.

But hunting and fishing are not only amusements of

the rich. They are also practiced by peasants seeking to enrich and

diversify their diet and, above all, by professionals who supply birds and fish to the popula-

tion at large and to poultry farms. These "hen houses" are, in fact, filled with wild birds like

ducks and geese that are kept for their eggs and meat but are not bred, so that the supply must constantly be

renewed. One time-honored method of bird hunting, used throughout Pharaonic times and even more recently

in some areas of Europe, involves using decoys to attract birds and then catching them with nets. The nets are

set around a marsh and hooked up so they can be quickly closed using a system of ropes. A domesticated bird

is set out on the water as a decoy to lure the wild birds into the area of the nets;

the hunter hides behind a screen of reeds and waits.

When enough birds have landed on the water near the

"traitor," the hunter yanks the rope and the net falls, after which he must

only retrieve the captive and overly trustful birds.

DEATH, THE TRIP THAT TAKES A LIFETIME OF PREPARATION

"Death lies before me on this day,
Like the perfume of the lotus,
Like dangling on the shore of ecstasy.

. . .

Death lies before me on this day,
Like the longing to return home,
After spending many years imprisoned."

This is how a man speaks to his soul more than five centuries before the reign of Ramses II. The Egyptians have made death into a second life, a true resurrection. A fragment of the texts carved on pyramids of the VI Dynasty, 2,200 years before the birth of Jesus Christ and 1,000 years before Ramses II, already proclaimed: "Go, so that you will return! Sleep, so that you will awake! Die, so that you might live!" For this second life, an Egyptian must prepare throughout his lifetime, commissioning the digging of a tomb and providing all the necessary things required after death so that he will live again within a familiar environment. The pharaoh must be buried with sumptuous funerary trappings, as indicated by all the goods piled up in the tomb of Tutankhamun; however, even "average" individuals don't leave without well-packed luggage.

In the tomb of the architect Kha, a tomb that has been found intact and unplundered, archaeologists have discovered the following objects:

Three sarcophagi, one placed within the other, for Kha and his spouse.

A small statue of the deceased, a copy of the *Book of the Dead*, and two *shawabty* (small funerary statues of servants intended to carry out the work that will be required of the deceased in the other world).

A chest containing Kha's articles, including five razors, pincers, a sharpening stone, a jar with pomade, a wooden comb, tubes made of tin, a flask with attached strap, a silver cup, a silver strainer and a copper one, two complete scribe pallets, four pestles to grind paints, a wooden stucco tablet for writing, a folding cubit (a kind of graded ruler), a scale and weights, a small carpenter's axe, a bronze scalpel, and three pairs of leather sandals. There were also a travel mat, two walking sticks, a casket with toiletry items, a casket with undergarments (50 pants, 26 shorts, 17 summer tunics, a winter tunic, and four pieces of linen).

His wife's wardrobe contained a wig with its storage box, bronze needles, hairpins made of bone, a wooden comb, a fringed dressing-gown, alabaster perfume vases, vases made of silver, glass, and so on.

The tomb furniture consisted of a high-backed chair, ten small stools, two little wooden tables, two beds with head-rests, and thirteen chests.

Various supplies were also placed in the tomb: bread, wine, oil, milk, flour, grilled and salted birds, salted meat, dried fish, green vegetables, onions, garlic, caraway seeds, juniper, dates, figs, and palm nuts. There were even gifts from the king: a silver seal and a cubit made of gold-plated wood.

GRAND
HOTEL
TAHRIR

CRUISE
PI-RAMSES/THEBES
HOTEL BOAT
-NEFERTARI-

DIPLOMATIC
LUGGAGE

HOTEL OF DEIR
EL-BAHARI
Dormitory
Tranquility
Guaranteed

DOMESTIC CUSTOMS
DRIED
FISH

RAMSES, A CORPSE BITTEN

While he wasn't the greatest Egyptian pharaoh in terms of military deeds or the extent of his conquests, Ramses II has certainly been the most avid traveler of all, especially after his death. Like any pharaoh, his first voyage brings him to his tomb, where his mummified body is laid to rest for all eternity, while his deified spirit sets off to join the sun-god Ra and to accompany him in his boat during his daily and nightly trips. Unfortunately, the sad realities of this world make eternity quite brief: like those of his predecessors and successors, the tomb of Ramses in the Valley of the Kings is looted, and his mortal remains are moved many times before reaching an undignified hiding place dug in the rocky cliffs of Deir el-Bahari. There, his mummy is stored haphazardly among those of many other Egyptian rulers.

Modern times prove just as cruel as antiquity, for at the end of the nineteenth century thieves discover this incredible assembly of pharaohs and queens of the New Kingdom. The looting starts again, but with it comes the potential for resurrection, for archaeologists hear about the discovery and in 1881 set about bringing the treasures to Cairo. The bureaucracy interferes, customs officials go crazy, so during their transport to Cairo the royal mum-

HOTEL
GIZA

CHAILLOT
CLINIC
GENERAL MEDICINES
DERMATOLOGY

HOTEL
MILAN

GRAND HOTEL
OF THE
VALLEY OF THE KINGS
SUITE 7

GRAND HOTEL
OF THE
VALLEY OF THE KINGS
SUITE 17

PI-RAMSES
PALACE
HOTEL

BY THE TRAVEL BUG

mies end up being registered under the category of "dried fish." Since then, crowds of tourists have been able to con-
template the faces of the greatest pharaohs in halls that have been consecrated to them. And the most celebrated of
these is Ramses II.

His popularity is such that an exhibition is dedicated to him in 1976. The organizers want to do more than bring
together objects from his period—they also want his mummy for the show. This leads to controversy, especially
since the mummy of Ramses II is in a poor state of preservation. In the end, the body of the king is sent to France
for special treatment. The precious mortal remains can thus be preserved without being exposed to the morbid and
disrespectful curiosity of visitors. In this way Ramses' body, whose spirit traverses the sky each day in the boat of
the sun, crosses the air in an airplane and is welcomed at Bourget airport in Paris with the honors usually
accorded a head of state: a band, military honor guard, and even the French secretary of state, who undoubtedly is
quite frustrated at not being able to shake hands with this important guest for the reporters' cameras.

The rediscovery of ancient Egypt began in the sixteenth century with tales told by travelers and renewed interest in Egyptian monuments and Egyptian-style monuments from imperial Rome. In the eighteenth century the fanaticism of some collectors launched a fashion for Egyptian items that extended to the realm of interior decoration. Napoleon's expedition to Egypt in 1798-99 coincided with the birth of the science archaeology, leading to a passion for things Egyptian that invaded all areas of artistic

EGYPT INVADES THE WESTERN MIND

endeavor, from architecture to painting and the minor arts, in a style that came to be known as Egyptian Revival. This reached a height during the glorious period of "Egyptomania," but the taste for Egyptian style has never waned and shows up in advertisements, clothing styles, and even popular music. The painting *Ramses in His Harem* evokes this fascination with the voluptuous East, with its harems and the glories of the days of the pharaohs. The so-called fountain of the fellah (a *fellah* is an Arab laborer) on Paris's Rue de Sèvres is a copy of a statue of Antinoüs (the favorite of Emperor Hadrian who drowned in the Nile) that was found in Hadrian's Villa.

Fountain in Rue de Sèvres (the so-called fountain of the fellah, or water carrier)

Ramses in His Harem

RAMSES II IN PARIS

"If an Egyptian obelisk is to be seen in Paris, it should be one of the two from Luxor . . . and as far as I'm concerned, it should be the one on the right, for reasons well known to me, although its pyramidal top is broken and it's shorter than its neighbor," wrote Jean-François Champollion to his brother on July 4, 1829. The idea had been circulating for over a year, ever since the pasha of Egypt, Muhammad Ali, had offered to donate to France one of the two obelisks from Alexandria, popularly known as Cleopatra's Needles. Champollion's wish was fulfilled, for on November 29, 1830, Muhammad Ali offered France one of Cleopatra's Needles as well as the two obelisks from Luxor. For financial reasons, the French did not take advantage of the pasha's generosity and were satisfied with only the western obelisk from Luxor, the one that Champollion had chosen. Sadly, he didn't live to see it erected under the sky of Paris. By the time the obelisk was set up in the Place de la Concorde, on October 25, 1836, the man who deciphered hieroglyphs had been dead for more than four years. (Incidentally, one of Cleopatra's Needles ended up in New York, the other in London.) Could Ramses II have imagined that the stone monument he had put in place in front of the temple of Luxor, its gold-covered top shining with the brilliant reflections of the sun-god's rays, would one day cross a vast sea to be erected in a country whose existence was unknown to him? Did he foresee that nearly 3,200 years after his death, his mummified body would pass by the foot of this monument under a gray and foreign sky? But then one of the inscriptions on the obelisk proclaims: "As long as the sky exists, your monuments also will exist, and your name will endure, as solid as the sky."

INDEX

BOOKS FOR FURTHER READING

Baines, John, and Malek, Jaromir. *Atlas of Ancient Egypt.* New York: Facts on File, 1981.

Bleiberg, Edward, and Freed, Rita, eds. *Fragments of a Shattered Visage: Proceedings of the International Symposium on Ramesses II.* Memphis: Memphis State University Institute for Egyptian Art and Archaeology, 1993.

Brown, Dale, ed. *Ramses II: Magnificence on the Nile.* Alexandria, Va.: Time-Life, 1993.

Budge, E. A., ed. *The Book of the Dead.* New York: Random House, 1994.

———. *The Rosetta Stone.* New York: Dover, 1989.

Gardiner, Alan H. *Egypt of the Pharaohs: An Introduction.* Oxford: Oxford University Press, 1966.

Hart, George. *Ancient Egypt* (Eyewitness Books). New York: Knopf, 1990.

Kitchen, K. A. *Pharaoh Triumphant: The Life and Times of Rameses II.* London: Warminster, 1982.

Macauley, David. *Pyramid.* Boston: Houghton Mifflin, 1975.

Mertz, Barbara. *Red Land, Black Land: Daily Life in Ancient Egypt.* New York: Peter Bedrick Books, 1990.

Putnam, James. *Pyramid* (Eyewitness Books). New York: Knopf, 1994.

Quirke, Stephen, and Spencer, Jeffrey, eds. *The British Museum Book of Ancient Egypt.* New York: Thames and Hudson, 1992.

Sabbahy, Lisa K. *Ramses II, The Pharaoh and His Time: Exhibition Catalog.* Edited by G. Wilfred Griggs. Jacksonville, Fl.: Jacksonville Art Museum, 1986.

Simpson, William K. *The Literature of Ancient Egypt.* New Haven: Yale University Press, 1973.

Sullivan, Richard. *The Story of Ramses.* Lewiston, N.Y.: Edwin Mellen Press, 1986.

Velikovsky, Immanuel. *Ramses II and His Time.* Cutchogue, N.Y.: Buccaneer Books, 1993.

ILLUSTRATIONS

© ACR, Édition Internationale, Bridgman: 46-47
Gilles Bachelet: 16-17, 64-65, 66-67
Michel Coudeyre: 32-33, 58-59
Thierry Dedieu: 90-91
© 1995, Éditions Albert René/Goscinny-Uderzo: 48-49
Françoise: 50
Jean-Claude Golvin, © Éditions Errance: 42-43
Jean-Claude Golvin, © Presses du CNRS: 62-63
Jean Henry: cover (retouching)
Daniel Kerleroux: 14-15, 72-73
Philippe Lagautrière: 70-71
Lecomte Du Noüy, © The Fine Arts Society: 92-93
Gérard Nicolas: 6-7, 68-69
© Oprey Publishing, Angus McBride in *Ancient Armies of the Middle East*, Terence Wise, Men-at-Arms Series: 24-25
Poncet de la Grave: 78-79
Michaël Welply: 10-11, 12-13

Neil Wilson: 30-31
Weber: 36-37

PHOTO CREDITS

Blaise Arnold: 22-23, 34-35, 38-39, 40-41, 54-55, 82-83, 84-85, 93
© Artephot: 8, 30-31
© British Museum: 56-57
© Ciné Plus: 26
© Cliché Musée de la Marine, Paris: 94-95
Michel Coudeyre: 52-53
© Photo RMN: 20, 53, 80-81, 89
Pix © Michael Freeman: 44-45
© TFI/Sygma: 60-61
Photos DR: cover, 4-5, 9, 74-75, 86-87
H. Gauthier, *Livre des rois d'Égypte*, volume 3, 1913: 18
Sir Alan Gardiner, *Egyptian Grammar*, Oxford University Press, 1969: 50-51
Stéphanie Bey: styling on 34-35, 38-39, 54-55, 84-85

DATE DUE

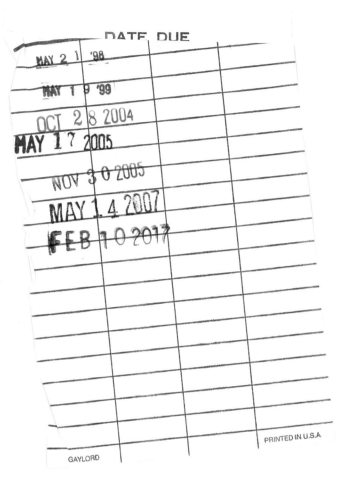

MAY 2 1 '98

MAY 1 9 '99

OCT 2 8 2004

MAY 1 7 2005

NOV 3 0 2005

MAY 1 4 2007

FEB 1 0 2017

GAYLORD   PRINTED IN U.S.A.